Very best wishes,

snow on willow

a nisei memoir

jean oda moy

jean oda moy

ISBN: I-4392-3637-2
ISBN-I3: 9781439236376

Visit www.booksurge.com to order additional copies.

By The Same Author

Literary Translations
Japanese to English

Tun Huang

Chronicle of my Mother

Shirobamba: A Childhood in Old Japan

All titles above by Yasushi Inoue,
One of Japan's foremost twentieth century writers

ACKNOWLEDGEMENTS

Initially, I planned to write a family history for my two children, but before I knew it this book emerged. My gratitude to Sylvia Halloran, our writing instructor, for creating a nurturing and validating environment in which I felt free to make mistakes and safe enough to reveal painful episodes in my life. The unstinting encouragement and enthusiastic feedback of my classmates gave me the incentive to expand and complete this memoir. Thanks to all.

I am also deeply indebted to my friend and editor, Carole Norton, whose invaluable suggestions, professional advice and incisive critiques helped bring this to fruition.

I have changed some of the names of individuals to protect their privacy.

Jean Oda Moy
2009

For Peter and Terry

Snow on willow
Branch bends
But does not break.

Japanese Proverb

CONTENTS

Prologue...I

I. My Family of Origin..5

    1. My Father, Yasukichi Oda 7

    2. My Mother, Chieko, A Picture Bride 13

    3. On to America..21

II. Life in America...27

    4. Sacrificial Lambs 29

    5. Three Little Cubs....................................33

    6. Into the *Yakuza's* Den.............................39

    7. West Seattle 43

    8. The Day My Brothers Left 49

    9. Maryknoll 53

    10. Survival As An Only Child.....................61

    11. Fun Times..69

    12. "No Japs Allowed" 79

III. Life in Wartime Japan 83

    13. Culture Shock......................................85

    14. Pearl Harbor Day in Japan....................95

    15. *Sennin Bari*..101

    16. Tokyo Rose...111

    17. Sweet Rain..115

    18. Escape..119

19. I Walked a Little.. 125

20. The Aftermath.. 131

21. *Pan-Pan* 143

22. "I'll Never Come Back"................................... 147

IV. Return to America 151

23. Hawaii 153
24. An Unconventional Arrangement 163
25. Long Island Hospital...................................... 169
26. A Detour Route to College 175
27. Boston University 183
28. The Social Whirl... 191
29. On to Brandeis 199
30. Only in America.. 207

Epilogue...215

PROLOGUE

Snow on Willow: A Nisei Memoir, is the story of my life as an American-born daughter of Japanese immigrants. My paternal grandparents, Fude and Rikiya Oda, emigrated from Japan to Hawaii in the late 1890s, leaving behind their young son, my father Yasukichi, in the care of his grandmother. Unfortunately, his mother died before Yasukichi could join his family in Hilo, and it was over a decade after his parents left that he was reunited with his father. He stayed in Hawaii just long enough to learn some English, then traveled alone to the U.S. mainland. When he was well established as foreman in a lumber company in the state of Washington, he married my mother, a "picture bride" from his home village.

I spent my early childhood years exposed to two cultures in pre-war Washington state. When U.S. anti-Japanese sentiments escalated in the 1930s, I was jeered at, called "Jap" and told "Go back home." At the same time, my mother and I dealt with fear and shame because of our not-so-secret "family secret," my father's alcoholism and domestic violence. Sensing the imminence of open hostilities between the United States and Japan, my parents took me with them to their homeland. In Japan I again experienced discrimination, this time partly because I was not fluent in Japanese, and partly because of anti-American sentiment. In school I was derided as "Yankee Girl" and treated like a social leper.

During the war years that followed, my family and I lived through terrifying air raids, severe food shortages and many other wartime hardships. At the moment when the first A-bomb fell, we were about 40 miles from Hiroshima and felt the massive jolt of the detonation. After the war, I worked two years for the U.S. occupation forces until I was able to obtain a passport to go back to the land of my birth. I then traveled alone to Boston, where I hoped to enter college. There, after much hard work at various jobs, plus generous scholarships, I managed at last to graduate from Brandeis University.

Much has been written about the incarceration and shabby treatment meted out by the U.S. government during World War II to some 120,000 people of Japanese ancestry rounded up on the West Coast. Very little is known, however, about the 15,000 to 20,000 American-born Japanese stranded in Japan during that time. I believe this is one of the very few books describing life in wartime and post-war Japan from the point of view of a young Nisei woman.

Although bigotry and prejudice against the Japanese were always part of my early awareness, my first fourteen years seemed quite removed from the larger world. We Nisei youngsters had many adventures in West Seattle, and I am filled with nostalgia when I recall my bountiful childhood with friends in our Japanese settlement there. In these pages I describe in detail some of those adventures. I also recollect long gone cultural events and traditions observed in that community, when life was uncomplicated and we reveled in simple pleasures without fear of harm from strangers. Sadly, that world and that lifestyle now exist only in my memory.

After the move to Japan, the hostility, suspicion and negative attitudes of those in my immediate social sphere seemed to constrict me to the point of psychic suffocation. Those were horrific years, the worst of my life, and they left scars. For many decades afterward, I repressed memories of that era, but as I wrote this memoir more and more "forgotten" incidents began surfacing. Now I am surprised and pleased to report that I can consciously view those experiences, mostly without pain. For I recall that during times when I struggled with and confronted the biased treatment I encountered on both sides of the Pacific, I formulated a vow to defy my detractors. I would not let them crush my spirit; rather, I would suppress my anger and use it to show them I was a lot better than they knew. That resolve undoubtedly helped me surmount numerous challenges and hurdles. And like willow branches in the falling snow, I would bend but would not break under the weight.

I.

MY FAMILY OF ORIGIN

I

MY FATHER, YASUKICHI ODA

Yasukichi was a holy terror. After his parents took off for Hawaii and left him behind in the care of his paternal grandmother, he turned unruly and aggressive, picking fights with other boys, cutting school, talking back to adults, and in general making a nuisance of himself. His grandmother could find no way to control him, so he did much as he pleased. And when villagers saw him coming, they would shout, "Here comes Yasu-u-u!" and quickly step aside to give him and the gang of urchins who ran with him a wide berth. My guess is that, at heart, he was a profoundly sad and lonely boy who was acting out because he missed his parents and felt abandoned.

His father, Rikiya, had gotten into a terrible brawl with one of his siblings after a night of heavy drinking and had landed in jail. Such altercations were by no means rare, and could be tolerated within the family. But for a family member to be incarcerated for any reason was an insufferable disgrace, and the entire clan was in an uproar. A meeting of the extended family was called to decide the fate of its incorrigible, and all agreed that Rikiya must be banished to Hawaii, where he could misbehave without further dishonoring the Oda name.

Since not even Rikiya could undertake to battle the whole clan, he reluctantly complied and went with his wife Fude to Hawaii. All this took place in the late 1890s. The couple had decided to leave seven-year-old Yasukichi in the temporary care of his paternal grandmother, because he would be a hindrance while they established themselves overseas. They planned to send for him later.

Although Rikiya's family were not of the higher ranks, they nonetheless *were* samurai.[1] Hence he considered himself above the physical labor of a common plantation worker. At the same time he was an enterprising sort. Once in Hilo he chose to start a one-man hansom cab operation, the first to be run by a Japanese in Hilo. He then sent his wife out to work as housekeeper for a German plantation overseer. This man ravaged her, and in consequence she produced a *happa-haole* (half-Caucasion) child. Rikiya's subsequent assaultive behavior would combine with physical complications following the child's delivery to hasten her end. On March 26, 1901, when the baby, who was named John, was a little over a year old and Yasukichi was almost 10, their mother died.

After Fude's death Rikiya began taking the baby along as he worked, carrying him in the folds of his kimono—the Japanese immigrants still wore kimono at that time in Hawaii—and even letting the child suck at his nipples when it grew fretful. According to my father's cousin, Kimiyo Yoshino, a young woman living in Hilo at the time, a firm bond developed between man and boy

---

1. The Oda clan, retainers of the Lord Murakami of Iyo Province (renamed Ehime-ken), moved in the early 1600s from Iyo on Shikoku Island to Hyugado-mari, a hamlet on the southeastern tip of Suo Oshima Island in Yamaguchi Prefecture. There they served their samurai lord as lookouts, or sentries of the sea, observing ships that sailed between the two islands on the Seto Inland Sea, for pirates were known to invade villages and hamlets in the area. The distance separating the two islands was about 15 miles. In addition to their sentry duties, the Oda men maintained livelihoods as fishermen. Miyamoto, Joichi, *My Japan Map, Seto Inland Sea III, Suo Oshima*, Doyu Kan, Tokyo, 1981.

even though Rikiya's parenting was a haphazard affair punctuated with frequent drinking bouts. Eventually Rikiya grew so fond of little John that he went so far as to enter his name in the family registry in Japan as *Masao Oda*, thereby acknowledging him as his own son. At that time Japan claimed all overseas residents and their children as Japanese citizens: all a man had to do was write to the appropriate village, town or city hall to register his overseas children. Because John looked different from other children and did not have a mother, he was mercilessly teased and tormented by some neighbors as well as by schoolmates. Yet somehow he managed to survive that life and even to thrive, for he was endowed with a lively, inquisitive mind.

Back in Japan, although Yasukichi's grandmother informed him about his mother's death, he would not learn of the existence of his *happa-haole* half-brother until much later. Meanwhile, with no one to encourage him, Yasukichi lacked incentive to do well in his studies. Despite his attitude and spotty school attendance, however (he often went fishing or looking for *mejiro* songbirds to cage), he managed in the spring of 1906 to obtain a certificate of graduation from his eight-year elementary school. He thereupon wrote to his father, Rikiya, to ask for passage money so he could go to Hilo to join him. Three years were to elapse before the money arrived: Rikiya repeatedly resolved to save his money, only to sabotage his plan with drinking and gambling.

When Yasukichi finally did arrive in Hilo, in 1909, his *happa haole* brother was ecstatic. Yasukichi was then eighteen, John nine. John saw in his older brother a possible ally and protector from their father's drunken rages, as well as from schoolyard bullies and neighborhood tormenters. Yasukichi, for his part, felt deeply disappointed that Rikiya did not welcome him as warmly as he had hoped and was more than a little chagrined that his father clearly favored John, who so obviously was not even his own son. And although Yasukichi was not unkind to John, he felt no particular sibling bond. His own first priority was to find work and make

Yasukichi (18) snd John (9) 1910

sense of his confusing new world. Thus he did not pay much attention to John's hopes and needs.

Yasukichi, as it turned out, was blessed with enough intelligence and native shrewdness that he quickly acquired skills to serve as a clerk at a relative's grocery shop. He worked there for more than two years, and during that time became moderately proficient in spoken English as well as a keen observer of the ways of the people around him. At just about that time a catastrophic fire destroyed all the Honolulu City Hall records, and Yasukichi took advantage of the situation to claim he had been born there. (He may have known that this was how many Chinese in San Francisco seized American citizenship after that city's vital records went up in smoke in the days following the Great Earthquake of 1906.) His aim was to move on to America. At that time, 1912, native-born Japanese could not enter the United States directly from the territory of Hawaii, but Hawaiian-born *Nisei* (second generation Japanese) could do so. Yasukichi succeeded in his claim and was approved for U.S. immigration.

John was devastated to learn his brother planned to leave, but Yasukichi consoled him with the promise that he would send the boy a bicycle when he saved up the money. Decades later a 94-year-old Uncle John plaintively told me: "I waited and waited and waited, but the bicycle never arrived."

In 1912 Yasukichi traveled to Seattle, Washington, where he soon found employment as an interpreter at a logging company. The lumber industry was booming in the Northwest, and hundreds of recent immigrants from Japan were making their way to the area in search of work. Few could speak English, and Yasukichi's services were in high demand. He soon advanced to a supervisory position.

Perhaps it was thanks to his samurai forebears that Yasukichi possessed such dauntless initiative. After leaving the logging company, he went gold mining in Alaska. He also did a stint in the U.S. Coast Guard—perhaps at some time when he was between jobs. In any case, our family album once contained many photographs of him posing on the deck of a Coast Guard vessel, spruce and cocky in his uniform.

One day after Father's death in January 1960, in a fit of pique, Mother burned all those pictures as well as the only photograph of his parents. She laughed as she told me how she had destroyed the pictures. She herself was recovering from surgery and radiation for uterine cancer at the time. "My friends predicted that I would die or become brain-damaged from his beatings," she said. "And even though I was sick at the time I was so angry I felt I just *had* to outlive that man; that would be my revenge." She sighed deeply, turned pensive then smiled. "I endured and endured and endured, and I finally won!" So it was that all pictorial evidence of Father as Coast Guardsman, like the Honolulu City Hall records, went up in flames.

2

MY MOTHER, CHIEKO, A PICTURE BRIDE

"We would like to have your daughter Chieko for Yasukichi's bride." An Oda clan member, acting as go-between, made this formal request of Chieko's father, Yukuji Nakamoto. It was common practice in the early twentieth century for immigrant Japanese men in Hawaii and America to write to relatives in their home villages to have women sent to marry them. After a likely candidate was found, photographs were exchanged. If both parties agreed to the arrangement, the woman would go overseas to join her bridegroom. These women were known as "picture brides."

Yasukichi Oda (28) 1920

The matchmaker in this case had brought a picture of 28-year-old Yasukichi Oda. Chieko's father looked searchingly at the photograph. He saw a small, trim, well-featured young man who he thought *looked* affluent. What he said was: "We cannot let our Chieko marry someone so far from home. Besides, we have other offers to consider."

Chieko was the youngest of the five Nakamoto children. Both the eldest son and eldest daughter were already married. The second son had died in his teens; the third son, Minoru, and the second daughter, Chieko, still remained at home. By custom the eldest son, the married Hikotaro, also remained in the home with his wife, because he was obligated to carry on the family name and care for his parents in their old age. It was he who would inherit all the family wealth.

Chieko Nakamoto (16) in School Uniform

Tea was served and a few stilted pleasantries exchanged before the go-between left, but only after eliciting Yukuji's promise that he would at least consider the proposal. After he left the eldest son, Hikotaro said, "I knew this Yasukichi before he had any money and fine clothes. He was the leader of that unruly pack of brats from Hyogadomari, the little hamlet east of here. I am definitely against our Chieko's getting involved with such a ruffian."

Chieko, then 16 years of age, was the pet of the family. When she was an infant her mother, Komu, could not bear to carry her in the traditional way of Japanese mothers, strapped on her back, because she could not see the baby's little face. She had always doted on the child, as had the rest of the family. When Chieko was still very young, a nursemaid was hired to care for her so that Komu could help with the family boat-building business. The wooden boats they built were used primarily for inter-island trade, although some were sturdy enough to travel to the South Sea Islands. One of

Komu's tasks was to serve tea and sweets to the boatyard workers during their morning and afternoon breaks. She was a very frugal woman who made her own *miso* (soy bean paste), pickles, and various condiments so the family would not have to purchase them.

As was the custom on Suo Oshima Island, Komu also wove *ikat* material into kimono for her family. In her later years my mother told me of a time when she sulked and threw a tantrumm because her mother refused to buy her a kimono from the village store. "Now I realize how much trouble she took to make a kimono for me," Mother said. "She bought white thread, took it to the indigo dyer to be dyed to specification in different shades of blue, then wove it into the intricately patterned ikat from which she sewed her kimono. It took her days to make a single kimono. How spoiled and ungrateful I was!" Mother sighed, then continued her recollections: "The only time Father ever scolded me was when I forgot to polish the oil lamps with old newspapers. That was my only chore, and I'd forget to do it."

She rambled on: "Brother Hikotaro often distracted me at mealtimes and—while I looked elsewhere—he sneaked morsels of my favorite foods onto my plate. Everyone was so good to me." She sighed again and smiled wistfully. "And in the springtime the hills above the village were dotted with brilliant red azaleas, and lavender and white wisteria wove their tendrils around the pine trees. And, oh, how the skylarks flitted up and filled the skies. How peaceful life was back then."

Although Komu deferred to her husband in public, she in fact ruled the roost in the home. Yukuji had joined her family in marriage and taken on her surname, in accord with the then prevailing custom for a family with an only daughter and no sons. The family formally adopted the daughter's husband as a member, in order to carry on the family name. Yukuji, for his part, had been orphaned early and was moreover a younger son with no prospect of inheritance; this marriage into the Nakamoto family gave him access to enough capital to start his own business. Also, Komu was truly smitten with him, for among other desirable qualities he was quite handsome, whereas she herself was rather uncomely. He was also a master boatwright, and as his business grew and prospered the Nakamoto household lived a most secure and comfortable life.

But around the time of Yasukichi's marriage proposal, Yukuji's business had fallen on hard times. He had contracted to build a large boat for a group of people who planned to sail on their own from Japan to the Hawaiian Islands. Then, when a major economic depression hit post-World War I Japan, the buyers cancelled their order. By this time Yukuji had already sunk much capital into the venture and owed money to the suppliers and to his men. How could he possibly pay his debts? He was overwhelmed by this reversal, and distraught with worry.

His younger son Minoru and his daughter Chieko in turn were frantic with concern that their father might take his own life. It was not uncommon for men in desperate financial straits to commit suicide rather than face public disgrace.

Chieko whispered to Minoru, "Do you think Father will kill himself?"

"He might drink that drafting ink," Minoru suggested. "It's supposed to be poisonous." They wept and clung to each other.

"I have an idea," Chieko told her brother. "I'll marry that rich man in America and send money home after I get there." Chieko had been raised on the Confucian precept for a woman: In childhood submit to your father, in marriage follow your husband, and in old age listen to your son. As a devoted daughter, she felt it only natural that she should try to help her family now. It was her filial duty.

Just that March she had graduated from Matsuyama Girls' High School on Shikoku Island, where the emphasis was on domestic arts. As a boarding student, she had attended classes in sewing, embroidery, cooking, tea ceremony, floral arrangements, *koto* (stringed instrument), and even a course on "how to massage your future mother-in-law's shoulders." A smattering of academic subjects was also offered and among these Chieko was particularly fond of European literature. She had read Dostoevsky, Chekhov, Tolstoy, Ibsen and many other Western authors. In addition, the Blue Stocking Movement, an early women's rights group, had made a certain impression on the idealistic teen-aged Chieko, who was especially moved by the predicament of Ibsen's Nora in "A Doll's House."

Because she had excelled in her high school studies, Chieko's instructors recommended that she become a teacher. A country girl's highest aspiration in that era was to attend normal school. With the decline in her family's fortune, however, further education was no longer an option for her. Hence Chieko prepared for her trip to America to marry the "rich man" and save her family.[2]

The relationship between the Oda clan and the Nakamoto family was complex, typical in many ways of the wary ambivalence between the samurai and the merchant classes. Among commoners the samurai were the elite class, followed by the farmers, the artisans, and finally the merchants. Thus, the Odas considered themselves of much higher rank than the Nakamotos. My mother told me that when she was a little girl any wife of a samurai was addressed

---

2 Chieko's mother Komu was one of the wealthy Nakamotos, an heiress to a Nakamoto branch family. Theirs was a family that had lived for well over 300 years in Amafuri, a hamlet on the southeastern end of Suo Oshima Island, just on the other side of a small hill from Hyugadomari, the Oda family stronghold. From around the time of the Meiji Restoration (1868) when the emperor was returned to power, the Nakamoto clan had been fresh fish wholesalers. They gathered the catch from nearby islands and kept them alive in a large salt-water well, then sold the most perishable ones to retailers in the nearby towns of Mitsugahama on Shikoku Island or in Kusatsu City in Hiroshima Prefecture. They shipped the fish in greatest demand, such as sea bream, to Osaka, where they fetched top prices. Thus the family prospered, and by 1900 the Nakamotos were the wealthiest family in all of Towa-cho, a township which covered a large portion of the eastern section of the island, comprising many little hamlets and villages. Their fortunes began to decline, however, when motorized boats came into use for transporting fish, and they lost out to competitors. Miyamoto Joichi, *My Japan Map, Seto Inland Sea III, Suo Oshima*, Doyu Kan, Tokyo, 1981.

as "Ogo-sama" (My Lady), even though she might be quite poor. Samurai families were very proud of their lineage, regardless of their material status. On the other hand, my mother's own Naka-moto kin, who did not lack for creature comforts, looked down on the Oda clan who had their pride to cling to but not much else. Chieko's father Yukuji even had enough discretionary funds to indulge his passion for collecting antiques and contemporary objet's d'art.

After their business declined, members of the main Nakamoto family then emigrated to Hawaii where many of their descendents currently live on Maui; Mina Nakamoto, a branch family member, founded a successful department store in Hilo on the Big Island (Hawaii Island).

3

ON TO AMERICA

As the ship pulled out of Yokohama harbor Chieko could see Japan's majestic Fuji-san, the sacred mountain, shining above the clouds. Her brother Hikotaro had accompanied her from their country home to see her off safely. He bowed from the dock, and she responded with a deeper bow of love and respect. The ship steamed eastward from the harbor, and both Hikotaro and Mt. Fuji blurred in her vision, merging, juxtaposed in her mind's eye. It was then that the reality of her situation struck home. She was actually leaving her family and her country to join her fate with that of a stranger—a stranger of whom Hikotaro strongly disapproved. Until now the idea of her trip to America had been exciting—like a novel in which she would play the dauntless heroine. But she was simply a frightened and very young woman alone on the deck of an outbound ship.

Alone on ship's deck
I gaze and gaze
At the receding Fuji
Wondering if I will ever
See her again.[3]

Chieko and Brother Hikotaro 1920

That Pacific crossing in June of 1920 lasted three weeks on a relatively calm ocean. Because local Japaneese newspapers in America had published a report that U.S. Congress was about the

3 This verse was found among Chieko's personal effects after her death in March 1981.

pass the Japanese Exclusion Act to halt immigration, many Japanese were rushing to beat the deadline, and dozens of picture brides filled the ships' cabins. Chieko, one of the youngest at sixteen going on seventeen was told by the older women that she should take one of the upper berths. She complied willingly enough, for she knew she was not likely to become seasick. Those not incapacitated with motion sickness passed their time gossiping and sharing their hopes and dreams of America.

Some were fearful that their bridegroom might not be as he had represented himself; tales circulated of older men "borrowing" photos of younger, better-looking acquaintances for picture exchanges. When their women arrived in America and learned of the duplicity, they had to swallow feeling of betrayal and anger and settle for what fate and trickery brought them rather than return home and lose face. Besides, most of them could not afford the return fare.

The day before Chieko's ship was due to dock, Yasukichi drove to Seattle in his Model T Ford from Cosmopolis, where he was foreman at the local lumber company. To make sure he would be in time to meet Chieko when she arrived early the next morning, he stayed that night at a nearby hotel. In the morning he joined other Japanese men waiting at the dock for their brides. The men smoked, chatted and shuffled about restlessly. When the ship finally arrived, the women disembarked apprehensively, each clad in her finest kimono. The first to meet them at the end of the dock were officers of the Japanese Association wearing identifying white armbands, assigned to help the newcomers through immigration and customs procedures. Those whose papers were not in order or who failed the physical examination—usually owing to tuberculosis, hookworm or trachoma—were detained in special quarters.

Some time elapsed before the president of the Association called out the name of the first bride and her husband came forward to claim her. Presently, Yasukichi heard, "Oda Chieko, wife of

Oda Yasukichi." He stepped up, removed his hat as the others had done, and nodded wordlessly to Chieko. She bowed low,and murmured deferentially, *"Hajime mashite yoroshiku."* [4] Socially awkward and self-conscious, Yasukichi merely grunted, then said, "Come on, let's get going." Chieko, who had been steeped in the social niceties, was considerably taken aback by his coarse and abrupt manner.

She was slender and, at five feet two and one-half inches, tall for a women of her generation. In addition, with her puffed-up pompadour hairstyle and her *geta* (wooden clogs) she appeared taller still. Yasukichi, on the other hand, was small for a man—only five feet two inches—and appeared diminutive beside his stately bride. He was a bit of a dandy, dressed on this occasion in a custom-made suit set off by a gold pocket watch on a chain. And Chieko noted that his face matched the photograph the go-between had brought to her parents. So at least he was not an impostor.

There would be no formal marriage ceremony. Like most other Japanese immigrants, Yasukichi had notified his village registry office that Chieko's name should be entered in his family list, and this was sufficient to make her his legal wife. Now Yasukichi and Chieko gathered her few pieces of luggage and placed them in the back seat of the Model T. It was Chieko's first automobile ride, and it was a truly thrilling event. She could hardly believe that she was the wife of a man who actually *owned a car.* Even a jinriksha ride had been considered a luxury by her parents, and here she found herself propelled into the modern age. Only millionaires and important politicians owned cars in Japan!

When they arrived in Cosmopolis, they were greeted warmly by the Tanakas, an older Japanese couple who worked as housekeeper and gardener for Mr. Cooney, the owner of the Cosmopolis Lumber Company. Mrs. Tanaka served the newlyweds a special dinner she had prepared and said quietly to Chieko, "Tomorrow I'll

---

4 Our first meeting ",I beseech your good will," a formal greeting still used upon first meeting by all Japanese.

take you shopping for Western clothes. In America we do not wear kimono." She also assured Chieko that she would teach her American ways and help in any other way she could.

Chieko was relieved and grateful to meet a kindly compatriot who would help ease her transition into a new lifestyle. But she was somewhat puzzled by the obviously concerned and searching expression on Mrs. Tanaka's face whenever their eyes met. She was soon to learn the reason behind those glances.

II.

LIFE IN AMERICA

4

SACRIFICIAL LAMBS

For the first few days of their marriage Yasukichi was brusque with Chieko, but not unkind. Then the abuse began. Like his father Rikiya, Yasukichi drank heavily and, in drunken rages, verbally and physically abused anyone unlucky enough to be around him. Chieko now became his primary victim. He found fault with whatever she said or did. When she tried to defend herself, he accused her of condescension, and the more she tried to reason with him, the more violent he became. Confused and battered, she was at a loss as to how to deal with this unreasonable man. At one point she said to herself, "I"ll let myself become a fool and agree with whatever crazy thing he says and do whatever he wants, no matter how arbitrary his demands." That didn't work. She tried silence. That only incensed him further, and led him to goad her into arguments. Chieko felt trapped. As indeed she was, well and truly trapped, in a loveless marriage to a violent man in a foreign land. She could not go home to her parents, for had she not come to America to save them? What was she to do? She saw no option but to endure and continue to suffer assaults at her husband's hand.

Chieko soon found herself pregnant. Her first child, Misae Rose, was born April 11, 1921; Shizue May followed on May 15, 1922. The young mother naively hoped that fatherhood might temper Yasukichi's behavior, but that didn't happen. Even worse, she had to work outside the home and see to her little ones at the same time.

Initially, Chieko had pleaded with Yasukichi to allow her to take English lessons, but he adamantly refused. He directed her to work in the laborers' kitchen to cook Japanese food for the men and then made money by charging for her cooking services. He also received commissions from Japanese food suppliers in Seattle for doing business with them. In addition, he collected fifty cents every month from each of the workers he had brought into the company—something he considered his due because he did all the hiring and firing of Japanese men. According to Chieko, he was making between $800 and $1,000 a month in the early 1920s.

In the meantime, Chieko pondered how she might pry some of this money from Yasukichi to send to her parents. He kept a tight rein on his money, making her account for every cent she spent, so she knew it would not be an easy task. She finally came up with a plan that might appeal to his avarice. She told him it was difficult, if not impossible, for her to continue cooking for the men while caring for the two babies. Every day she was endangering their lives by bringing them to the kitchen, having them near the burning stove and hot pots and pans. Besides, she was distracted by their needs, and thus less efficient and productive than she might be. Wouldn't it be *financially* more rewarding to take the girls to her parents' home in Japan and send them a little money for their raising? That way she could earn much more for him by continuing to cook at the company. To her surprise, Yasukichi agreed without argument. It was probably easy for him to let go of his daughters, who were unimportant in the family system; sons would have been a different matter.

Thus in the fall of 1922 Chieko took her two daughters to Japan. Whether she realized it or not, she was offering them as sacrificial lambs on the two altars of her parents' financial need and her husband's greed and self-indulgence. She was first, last and always the filial daughter. Little Misae Rose was about a year and a half and Shizue May just several months old when they left for Japan. And Chieko herself was nineteen—still a teenager. I believe that Rose and May never did forgive their mother for abandoning them, for they were not made aware of her true circumstances in America.

Chieko managed to remain in Japan for several months before she reluctantly returned to her husband. She knew her parents could not afford to support her, and so once again she set forth for America to "save her family." But this time she knew full well what awaited her.

Father with Misae Rose, Mother with Shizue May, 1922

5

THREE LITTLE CUBS

After her agonizing separation from Rose and May in Japan, Chieko returned to America and bore three more children in quick succession. Frank Tsutomu arrived on November 11, 1924, followed by Jean Yasue on January 28, 1926, and finally John Yoneo on May 8, 1927. Frank's entrance into the world—the first-born son and heir—was heralded with great rejoicing. There is an extra large portrait of the laughing, naked infant Frank among our family pictures. My birth as the third daughter was no cause for celebration, just quiet acceptance. What is unusual, however, is the existence of a portrait of this "unimportant" year-old child. According to Mother, the photographer hired for our family portrait was so taken with me that he persuaded her to let him take of picture of me alone. When John came along as as backup heir, the family now seemed complete. Mother's French-born doctor suggested she have her tubes tied, and she readily agreed, for she did not want to bring any more children into such a chaotic home. That procedure strikes me as quite a sophisticated form of birth control for that era. She was not yet twenty-four.

Jean Yasue, 1-year-old, 1927

As far back as I can remember there were always the three of us—Frank, John and me. We did everything together; we played and fought, ate, bathed and slept together. And when Father started shouting, we huddled together and clung to each other. When I look back, I think of us as three frightened little cubs.

Mother converted to the Methodist faith and thereafter would leave Father for a Christian women's shelter several times when she could no longer bear his abuse. Each time, however, an intermediary, usually one of Father's co-workers or business associates, came to plead his case, saying that he promised to reform, and Mother would relent.

One time Mother left home without John. "I had to hold Frank's hand because he was only two and a half," she said to me later, "and you couldn't walk yet, so I had to carry you. I couldn't take all three of you, so I left John behind in his crib. I thought that Papa would not hurt an infant. But when I came back I found John beaten black and blue." I have often wondered whether that early trauma led to John's mental illness in later years.

On another occasion Mother said to me, "You know, you took your first steps in a women's shelter." I felt very sad to hear that such a joyful event was fated to take place in such an unhappy environment.

The childless Tanakas who had served Mother her first dinner in America were so concerned about her welfare and that of the children they were willing to brave Father's wrath by offering her a home and help with raising her children. They said to her, "Unless you leave him now, you don't know what he'll do to you and the children. Look what he did to John when you left him last time." Mother was grateful for their concern, but she knew that unless she stayed with Father she could not send money to her parents in Japan. And as she felt she just could not let them down, she reluctantly declined their generous offer.

Frank, Father, Jean, John, and Mother, 1929

Materially, Mother did not want for anything, for Father wanted others to see how prosperous he was. We lived in a two-story house, he bought a new car every year, and he attired her and the children in expensive clothes. He even purchased costly jewelry for her. His wife and children were his trophies. But his abuse continued. He was an unhappy, sadistic man, probably because he felt unloved. My guess is that he remained emotionally a child, and that he bullied everyone as an adult simply because he had the power to do so and because he knew no other way of relating.

In the late 1920s our family left Cosmopolis and moved from lumber camp to lumber camp while Father worked for Shafer Logging Company as a foreman supervising hundreds of Japanese laborers. The operations he oversaw were extensive, and Mr. Masato Terada became his co-foreman. In October 1984 I visited the Terada family in Seattle and gained some information about those years. Mr. Terada told me that there were camps in Oakville, Centralia, Montesano, and Saginaw, Washington. In Saginaw, the last camp they worked before the Great Depression, special houses were built for the Terada family and for our family. Mr. Terada boasted that the two foremen were the only ones allowed to wear pistols to keep the laborers under control, and they had permission to shoot the rebellious ones. I shuddered to think of Father carrying a gun. With his volatile temper it's a wonder that he didn't kill someone in a fit of rage. Or did he?

I have only fleeting, kaleidoscopic memories of my early years in the lumber camps—sitting on our dog's back, playing on the porch with my brothers, riding on a handcar, and watching the laborers go in and out of their freight-car dormitories.

Mother recalled an incident where a neighbor told her, "Your Jean is different from other children; she has a mind of her own. Although she's only two, she refused my help when I tried to pull up her pants. Instead, she clutched her pants with one hand and ran away from me. She's such an independent child." Mother looked pleased at the recollection, but I'm not sure whether her pleasure derived from my being called independent or because I ran home to her.

In spite of her many hardships, Mother never lost her love for nature. She often told of seeing salmon spawn in a river near one of the camps. "Can you imagine the hundreds upon hundreds of salmon swimming upstream? What an incredible sight! They glittered in the sun and were so numerous that sometimes they seemed to be swimming in layers. At times they even jumped up onto the riverbanks. I was simply awed by the power of nature." She smiled as she reminisced, and I believe that memories such as these—brief respites of sunshine peeping through clouds—helped sustain her in her darkest hours.

6

INTO THE YAKUZA'S DEN

As we all know, the stock market crash of October 1929 caused tsunami-like economic repercussions throughout the world. The Saginaw, Washington, lumber camp where Father worked somehow managed to survive for almost a year after the initial catastrophe, but it too finally folded in September 1930. Our family then moved to a house between Beacon and Eighteenth streets on the edge of Seattle's Japan Town. As soon as Mother learned there had been a suicide in the house, however, we quickly relocated to another place, on Washington Street, across from a pre-school run by a Japanese woman. I actually remember the spooky feeling in that first place.

According to Mr. Terada, family friend and Father's former co-foreman, Father had speculated heavily in the stock market during the boom years and lost a lot of money in the crash. He also continued to gamble and drink, so that by the time we reached Seattle he had squandered all but $10,000 of the family nest egg. And then, even though he was unemployed, he recklessly continued on his disastrous course, gambling away much of what was left.

Apparently Father had serious unpaid debts, for Mother learned that a contract on his life had been put out by the top yakuza (Japanese gang lord), Kimpachi Yamamoto, a man from Tosa, the province which reputedly produced rough, tough people. Kimpachi[5] was known to many as the man who controlled all Japanese gambling, prostitution, and other illegal activities on the West Coast from Seattle to Los Angeles. It was commonly said that he personally had killed at least eight times, boasting that killing people was "as easy as killing chickens." Mother told me that men were known to have entered his "office" and never been seen again. The rumor was that he disposed of his victims in his furnace, his very own crematorium. The authorities never bothered him.

Although no love was lost between my parents, Mother was frantic at the thought that Father could become Kimpachi's next statistic, for she needed his help to support the children and to send money to Japan. Thus she took an uncharacteristically audacious move that she told me about only years later.

"I took you with me to see Kimpachi," she finally told me, and I pleaded with him to spare Papa's life because he had five children dependent upon him and I needed his help to raise them.

I was so frightened that my whole body trembled. My voice cracked when I spoke, and I could hardly breathe. I felt so lightheaded I thought I might faint. And I hung on tightly to your hand to give me courage.

"After listening to me, he said, 'You're a brave woman to come here.' Then he dismissed me."

She added, "He must have cancelled the contract, because nothing happened."

When I heard this story I was incensed to learn that Mother would risk my life to save Father's. In retrospect I think she was so focused on the family's financial security—Father's earnings

---

5 *Yamada Waka Monogatari* (The Tales of Waka Yamada), an autobiography of the top bordello madame in Seattle in the early 1900s, is said to describe Kimpachi's dealings.

and/or loss thereof—that it probably didn't even occur to her that she was jeopardizing my safety. She had probably heard through the grapevine that Kimpachi also had a young daughter whom he loved, and probably she hoped to elicit his sympathy by bringing me with her. I was about four or five at the time. Mother's visit to the yakuza's den was successful, I suppose, but I'm glad I have no recollection of that event.

When I told Mr. Terada that Father had died in Japan of a brain tumor, he shook his head and said, "I never thought that man would die on the tatami." In other words, he would not have expected my father to die of natural causes.

7

WEST SEATTLE

"How old are you?" Mrs. Tsunoda, our new neighbor, asked me in Japanese.

"Pretty soon five." I replied in the broken English that I had recently acquired from my Nisei playmates in Seattle. Only Japanese was spoken in our home, but I liked to try out my new English vocabulary. My brothers Frank, six, and John, three, were also picking up English from their friends.

It was December 1930 and our family had moved again—this time to West Seattle, to a Japanese settlement that originated sometime during World War I. There was a shortage of labor in the local mills during those war years, and the owner of Nettleton Sawmill Company, located on a pier on Elliot Bay at the base of our hill, purchased the land and built two dormitories for his hard-working, unmarried Japanese employees. As the sawmill fortunes declined, one of the dormitories was razed, and Mr. Ishii, an original Issei (first generation immigrant) settler, built a two-story home from the scrap lumber. His was the first family to take up residence in the settlement and he would became the unofficial historian for that community. Thanks to the lovely setting, low rent, and bountiful seafood available for the taking, soon more homes were built, and other families from downtown Seattle moved into the area. At the time we moved in, there were seven other families, but at its peak the community comprised ten to twelve households. Over the years, as some families returned to Japan others moved in to take their place.

It is probable that Father had almost depleted our family savings by 1930, so the lower rent was an enticement, added to the fact that the homes were spaced far enough apart to provide privacy from prying neighbors' eyes during his drunken rampages. Another bonus for Father was that he could make his own sake without fear of official meddling. Prohibition was still in effect, and he had become something of an expert brewer. Now, after teaching Mother how to distill the sake from rice and malt in a large pantry off the kitchen, he soon delegated the project entirely to her, ensuring himself a steady supply of top-quality beverage, of which he drank about a quart a day.

While Father sat around drinking and brooding over his "bad fortune," Mother went to work at the California Bag Company, a factory that made gunnysacks. She hired Mrs. Ishii, wife of the would-be historian, to babysit Frank, John and me. Mrs. Ishii's youngest was still a toddler, and babysitting the young children of other mothers was her way of supplementing her family income. She was an aloof, unhappy woman enmeshed in a second marriage, with two children from her first marriage and two from the current one, plus two stepchildren she packed off to live with their relatives in Japan. She gave us minimal care: fed us lunch and let us play inside only when it rained (which of course was quite often in Seattle). Much of the time we children—hers and those she supervised—were left to our own devices. We often took turns swinging on the hammock that Father had hung between two trees in our side yard, pushing each other so wildly that the hammock usually overturned and the occupant landed smack on the ground. It's a wonder that none of us was seriously injured or killed, for we had many other adventures I now know were dangerous—climbing tall trees, jumping off the roof of a shed, playing on the shores of Elliot Bay. Buddha must have been looking after us.

At home Frank, John and I enjoyed the companionship of our gentle, protective German shepherd, Lady. When John wandered off by himself now and then, we usually found him asleep, with Lady standing guard. In those days most people did not spay or neuter their pets and Lady would deliver an annual litter, always to our great joy. I tried to dress the puppies in doll clothes, while Frank and John would place them in cardboard cartons and push them around the house. Lady seemed to know intuitively that we were harmless young children and let us have our way with her pups. One night as we slept, Father would put the puppies in a gunny sack and drown them in Elliot Bay near the lumber yard. When we woke to find "our babies" gone, we were heartbroken and moped about for days. This happened every year.

At one point Mother simply disappeared. Frank, John and I were frantic and searched for her everywhere. We went all over the house, checking even the closets, the pantry, and the extra storage room we never used. We went outside, to the front, back and sides of the house, calling "Mama! Mama!" But there was no reply. Then we visited all our neighbors to see whether she might be visiting one of them, but no one had seen her. We panicked. What would we ever do without our mother? Even Father was at a loss, for he was forced to look after three young children. Somehow he managed to feed us and parent us in his brusque fashion until Mother returned a few days later—probably from a Christian women's shelter. We three clung to her, crying, "Mama, please don't leave us again, please stay home with us!" Mother also wept. She just could not abandon her children completely, no matter what the cost to her. For a short while thereafter, Father was on his best behavior.

From the time our family moved to West Seattle, Mrs. Tsunoda had been particularly kind to me, inviting me into her home and plying me with all sorts of goodies and gifts. She wanted to adopt me. In those days, childless couples either adopted one of their relatives' children or one from a family with many children. The Tsunodas, as well as our other neighbors, probably knew how hard life was for my mother, and as I was the third daughter, they thought my parents might let me go. Mother, however, firmly refused, saying that each child was precious to her and she could not bear to give me away. For my part, I tried to imagine life with gentle, frail Mrs. Tsunoda as my new mother. She was the only woman I knew who did not work outside the home and who was supported by a solicitous, kind husband. Theirs appeared to be a peaceful, happy houseold, so unlike ours. But no amount of goodies could pry me away from my very own real mother, regardless of my fear of Father's behavior. I was glad Mother did not give me away.

For what felt like an eternity—though perhaps it was only a matter of months—Father refused to work at all and sat at home moping and drinking. At length Mother somehow managed to persuade him to seek any kind of employment, and he too started working at the bag company doing some menial task. This must have been a severe blow to his ego, but he insisted on driving to work in his old Chrysler, the last vestige of his former wealth. Once he started working, however, he was surprisingly sober and diligent on the job. Like many alcoholics, he then did his drinking only after hours.

How we dreaded those evening hours! Father's physical and verbal abuse escalated as he took out his frustrations on all of us. Many a night we went to bed hungry because one sweep of Father's arm across the table had sent our supper onto the kitchen floor. On a few occasions Frank dared not come home for fear of Father's wrath over some childish misdemeanor. Mother, John and I would search the whole neighborhood until we found him, shivering in some cold, dark hideaway. And I vividly recall holding my breath when Father once took a kitchen knife to John's wrist, threatening to cut off his hand. I remember wondering if Father would chop off his son's hand the way Mother chopped off a chicken thigh. Little John just sat stock still, merely watching until Father put away the knife. At times like that I curled myself into the fetal position or crept into another room—anything and everything to escape Father's attention. How I feared and hated that man!

8

THE DAY MY BROTHERS LEFT

Our family with Mr. Sakata, standing on right 1933

I shall never forget my mother's profound sadness on the day my brothers left for Japan. Frank, aged eight, and John, five, sailed out of

Seattle Harbor on the *Hikawa Maru* with Mr. Sakata, a family friend, who was to deliver them to our maternal grandparents. In a formal portrait commemorating the event, dated 1933, Father looks stern, Mother sad, Frank and I solemn, and little John happy and innocent.

For weeks before, whenever the Japan trip was mentioned I had cried and screamed, "I won't go! Please don't make me!" I am not sure now what frightened me, but I knew I didn't want to leave. Unlike my brothers, I was determined to stay with Mother. My unexpected outbursts alarmed her.

"It must be an omen that she will get sick and die if we force her to go," Mother said to Father, and they decided to keep me with them. I was a thin, frail child of seven.

Like so many other immigrant families in America, my parents had planned to return to the old country after they saved enough money. Therefore, they sent their children ahead to learn the language and culture. Ten years earlier, Mother had taken my two sisters to live with her parents in Fukuoka. Now, since I was the third daughter and the least important child according to the family system, my education was not considered as vital as that of my siblings. Besides, I believe Mother wanted to keep at least one child with her, and my protests gave her a convenient excuse.

At the dock, passengers and well-wishers shouted their farewells and took pictures. They tossed bright paper streamers back and forth. A kaleidescope of colors, a din of music and voices, and the tangy scent of the sea assailed our senses. Frank, caught up in the excitement, hurled tapes down to us. Some missed their mark and landed in the water. John crouched below the railing and stared intently at Mother's face. Frank handed him a few ribbons to hold.

Mother continued urging: "Frank, catch this one," or "Come, John, throw one to me."

Father did nothing. He stood beside her and watched. And I... I chased and picked up the rolls Frank tossed, handing some to Mother and keeping some for myself.

Then the crew raised the gangplank and the ship slowly glided off to the strains of "Auld Lang Syne." Mother unwound the tapes in her hand, holding onto these ties with her sons for as long as possible. As the ship gained speed, the paper strands separated, then fluttered down into the water. Tears rolled down Mother's cheeks, her chin quivered, and still she clutched the streamers in her hand. She made no sound. She just stood there, watching her little sons carried farther and farther away.

That night she took me to bed with her and held me all night. Her body shook and I knew she was weeping.

"Mama, please don't cry," I pleaded as I stroked and patted her, trying desperately to comfort her in the only way I knew.

"I shouldn't have let them go," she kept muttering to herself. And she sighed over and over again. Oh, how Mother sighed the night my brothers left tor Japan.

Frank Tsutomu, Grandfather, John Yoneo, Misae Rose, Grandmother, Shizue May 1933

9

MARYKNOLL

"Mama, I wish John and Frank were still here," I said one day shortly after my brothers left. Although I enjoyed being the center of Mother's attention, I missed the boys' companionship and even our fights.

"I know, I know." Mother turned away. Since parting with her sons, she doted on me as never before.

The next school year I entered second grade, and my parents transferred me from the local public school to a Catholic mission school. Maryknoll offered one hour of Japanese-language lessons every day, an experience my parents saw as one way to prepare me for our eventual return to Japan. They considered the legendary discipline of the nuns an additional bonus.

At first the school provided bus service to students living in outlying areas of the city—South Park, Beacon Hill and West Seattle. The bus went from house to house picking up students, and Brother Adrian, the driver, entertained us by telling jokes and singing. He often sang "The Object of My Affection" at the top of his lungs, to our great amusement. What he didn't realize was why we children snickered. We all knew that Brother Adrian "liked" Sister Mary Bernice, because we had seen them whispering and laughing together. My friend Anne told me she once caught them holding hands. It was a not-so-secret romance, for, like most youngsters, we did not miss much.

Unfortunately, the bus service was soon discontinued, and thereafter we riders had to get to school on our own. Since Maryknoll was located all the way across town from where I lived, several of the neighborhood children and I now commuted for an hour by streetcar and cable car to get there and another hour home. We transferred at Yesler Way, in the heart of downtown Skid Row, where drunks staggered on the streets and lay passed out on the sidewalks. Indian squaws huddled in doorways, wrapped in their blankets. In the middle of Pioneer Square an old man tended a tobacco and candy stand. Pigeon droppings were everywhere.

Once an inebriate singled me out and shouted, "Jap! You dirty Jap! Go back where you came from!" *I was born here, and I'm an American, too*, I thought bitterly. "I'd rather be a Jap than a sap, like you!" I yelled back. Then I ran as fast as I could to catch my cable car. When the motorman let me ring the warning bell at intersections, I tingled with pride, temporarily forgetting all my hurt and anger. I was nine or ten.

Maryknoll was established exclusively for Japanese-American boys and girls, both "heathens" and converts, and there we passed our days in cocoon-like insulation from the prejudices of the white world. It was a small school with twelve to thirteen students in each class from first through eighth grades, and some of the nuns ran their courses with Spartan rigor. Academic standards were high. From fifth grade on we dissected sentences grammatically, and in seventh grade we started on algebra. Students who had trouble with their lessons were kept after school day after day until the tenacious nuns who gave them individual tutoring were satisfied they had learned what they needed to know. Unlike the common practice of today, we were not automatically promoted; those who did not keep up or were out of school for long periods of time, either with illness or long vacations to Japan with their folks, were held back and made to repeat the grade.

Nutritious hot soup was offered for five cents a bowl, and sometimes the cook served macaroni and cheese, a great treat for those (most if not all of us) whose parents never cooked American-style food. Most of us usually brought sandwiches from home to go with the soup.

Annual Christmas pageants were produced in Japanese, to the parents' great delight. Our Japanese teachers coached us with the Nativity play, Japanese folk stories, and dances. I remember my part as the angel who brings "glad tidings" to Mary. We even sang "Silent Night" in Japanese. Most of us were not proficient in the language but managed to memorize our lines. After the pageant was over, we students walked through dark, unheated corridors to our icy class-rooms to see what Santa Claus had left at our desks. My friend Anne recalls being thrilled at receiving a double-decker pencil case with various implements. Another friend, Ida, remembers she was not particularly pleased with her gift of a Japanese doll, for she already owned similar dolls. For some reason, I have absolutely no recollection of any gifts I received or my reactions to them.

May Day was a very special day for us, for on that day Brother Charles and Brother Adrian drove two busloads of students—probably the whole student body—to the ferry landing. From there we took a boat across Lake Washington to St. Edwards Seminary in Kirkland. There we proudly walked and sang in a procession all around the grounds, the girls in white dresses and wearing white shoes. One of the girls would place a flower wreath on the head of Mary's statue, while the rest of us sang:

> Oh, Mary, we crown thee with blossoms today,
> Queen of the angels, queen of the May...

The nuns also took us on field trips to places they considered educational for us. At the Carnation Dairy Farm, we observed the milking and bottling processes, after which the dairy's staff treated us to delicious, creamy ice cream cones. On another occasion we went to a slaughterhouse on the outskirts of Seattle and watched as the workers, clad in heavy aprons, killed bawling steers by slitting their throats, sliced their carcasses into a variety of cuts, then ground the scraps and stuffed them into the animals' intestines to make sausages and frankfurters. The experience left most of us queasy, and I could not bear to eat hot dogs or my favorite sukiyaki meat for some time after that. Other outings were not quite so memorable.

Sister Mary Jane was the most feared nun of all, for she disciplined students for minor infractions with a sharp slap with a ruler on hands or wrists, or relegated the offender to the back of the chapel. I remember her calling me "lazy" because I rushed through my assignments and often did my homework at school to avoid carrying books home. She even sent me to the back of the chapel a few times for whispering in class and for chewing gum. Occasionally she administered a rough shaking to one of the boys. She was especially hard on boys, I noticed, and I wondered later whether she entered the convent because she disliked men. She was also a "fire and brimstone" lecturer, warning us often that on Judgment Day the whole world would see every one of our wicked deeds—on something resembling a movie screen, as I envisioned it. And on that day our true evil would come to light. None of us would be exempt from God's wrath. That horrifying scenario led me more than once to assess my myriad sins, both mortal and venial, and to conclude I would most certainly roast in Hell, no doubt about it.

On the other hand, we all loved Sister Mary Bernice, our third-grade teacher, because she was so much fun. Not only was she good at playing marbles, hopscotch and *jin-tori* (a Japanese war game in which each of two teams tries to capture the other's stronghold), but she could also run very fast. The crucifix she wore around her neck and the rosary at her waist swung back and forth and her veil flew behind her as she raced on. We were amazed that a nun could run at all. We were astounded. And she never used a ruler to discipline a student or spoke harshly in reprimand. It was as if she were one of us. I realize now that she was probably very young.

Fifth and Sixth Grade School Play
(Jean standing 2nd from left)

Sister Mary Carmel, our eighth-grade teacher, was a reserved, distant woman who moved with grace and dignity, and apparently came from a well-to-do family. She obviously had dance and piano lessons before entering the convent, for she taught us the minuet as well as balletic movements for our school plays. In addition to serving as our music teacher, she led us in choir practice, which we were all required to attend. There we learned to sing a Mass in Latin, which none of us understood. I was assigned to the alto section. I found singing in the choir a mesmerizing experience, what with the chanting by the priest and our responses, and some of the ritual aspects of the Mass felt deeply satisfying. But the long sermons were boring, and at times the overpowering scent of incense as the priest swung the censer back and forth made me feel giddy and ill.

My very favorite teacher was Sister Mary Edith, a pale, gentle soul with a dry sense of humor. One day Hideaki, a boy who often came up with impertinent questions, asked, "Sister Mary Edith, do you have hair under your veil?" Her eyes twinkled with amusement. "What do you think?" she said. She never did answer the question.

I was drawn to her because she did not proselytize like the others who tried to persuade me to enter the convent "because you are so good in catechism." Yes, certainly I could parrot back what I had read in the book, but I had no inclination—no "calling"—to become a nun. I was surprised at Sister Mary Edith's sensitivity and impressed with her emphasis on the secular arts.

She took a special interest in me, often encouraging me in private to read as much as possible. Since the school library was limited mostly to religious stories and Elsie Dinsmore-type books in which the heroines were always impeccably behaved girls who did the right thing, she suggested that I seek out the classics available at my local library. I had already obtained a card from the West Seattle Public Library a few years earlier, but until then my primary reading choices had been mostly fairy tales and animal stories. Under her tutelage, my range expanded to include Alcott, Dickens, Twain, Stevenson and Defoe. Mother was pleased to see me regularly bringing home books from the library, for she herself read Japanese literature far into the night.

When I graduated from Maryknoll, I asked Sister Mary Edith to sign my autograph book, as was the custom back then. Instead of the religious message I expected, she penned, "'To thine own self be true.' Hamlet." At the time I wasn't exactly sure what the words implied, but through the years that quotation from Shakespeare seemed to insinuate itself into my psyche as a sort of watchword.

Some of my recollections of other Maryknoll staff members—nuns, priests, Japanese teachers—have blurred and become merged in my memory bank. But as I reflect on those years, I am filled with nostalgia and gratitude for the love, dedication, scholastic excellence, and secure environment they provided for us. I realize now that those school years—from 1933 to 1940—were the happiest of my life. And though the nuns and priests failed to convert me to their religion, I shall always be proud to have been a Maryknoller.

10

SURVIVAL AS AN ONLY CHILD

An only child is often a lonely child—and that was the case for me. Now that my brothers were in Japan with our grandparents, I served as the single buffer between my parents. They often used me to communicate with each other: "Tell your mother this..." or "Tell your father that...." Thus, early on I learned well my role as peace-keeper. I often told Mother not to contradict Father and fuel his anger, and when Father picked a quarrel with Mother I glared and shouted, "Leave Mama alone!" Sometimes they listened to me, but most of the time they didn't. Then I felt helpless and powerless.

Father continued to get drunk and abuse Mother, and I did my best to protect her by wedging myself between them when his attacks became physical. Sometimes this tactic worked, but at other times he only became further incensed, pushed me aside, and esca-lated his assault. Once in a drunken rage he struck her on the head with some hard object and blood poured down her face. She cried out hysterically, "Kill me! Go ahead and kill me if you want!" Then she collapsed on the floor and sobbed. I frantically ran next door to get Mrs. Ishii. Father calmed down when she came to attend to Mother's injury. After that incident I felt certain that Father would kill Mother some day. In anticipation of that terrible possibility, I tried to persuade her to run away. "Let's go to California. I'll take you," I said. With all the naiveté of a 10-year-old, I sincerely thought I could somehow find a way to lead her to safety. She patted me on the head and turned away.

Some time after that, Father brought out carving knives and brandished them at Mother. This time she simply walked out the front door, saying to me, "Stay with him. He won't hurt you." For some reason Father never did beat me. Perhaps it was because I refused to cry at his rages and only stared at him, hiding my fear as well as I could. Or was it possible that he actually cared about me, that is, as much as he could ever care about anyone other than himself? I did not think it strange that Mother would leave me to placate him, for I considered it my clear duty to protect her. She returned a few hours later, and by then he had calmed down.

Father, Mother and Jean (10)

Whenever Father got drunk and demanded that I sit down and listen to him, I complied because I knew that as long as I allowed him to ramble on with one of his aimless, interminable "lectures" he would not hurt Mother. As I held in my own anger, though, my blood pressure must have soared for I had nosebleeds that took what felt like ages to control. Years later Mother laughed as she recalled those incidents. *Did she not realize I endured Father's crazy rantings for her sake?* I wondered, but I did not confront her, for by then she was an old woman.

Mother regularly indulged me in various ways. All my friends had chores at home, but she gave me none. "You'll have enough to do when you grow up and get married. Enjoy your childhood," she said. And she always cooked my favorite dishes, often watching me as I ate, opening her own mouth with each bite I took. Unlike other mothers, she never told me to clean my plate. She seemed grateful that I would eat what little I did. I was a finicky eater, thin as a rail and often ill with tonsillitis. Mother tried her best to fatten me up, even ordered a chocolate milk delivery when I refused to drink regular milk. Once, just to test her limits, I even refused to drink chocolate milk, saying, "I'll drink it if you pay me a nickel." And to my great surprise, she paid.

Mr. Senda, a Japan Town grocer, made weekly rounds of many outlying Japanese communities, including ours, to take orders for Japanese food—tofu, miso (soy bean paste), soy sauce, sukiyaki meat and other Japanese foods and condiments that we could not obtain locally. Later in the week he would deliver the orders, so we never lacked for any type of food we wanted.

The Issei always patronized Japanese-speaking professionals; thus, because of my frequent bouts of tonsillitis, my parents took me to a Japanese surgeon's office for a tonsillectomy. We later learned this surgeon had such a drug problem I was fortunate not to have died under his knife. When my permanent teeth grew in crooked, Mother consulted a dentist about the possibility of orthodontia for me. "It's important for a young girl to have straight teeth and look pretty," she said. The man told her we should wait a while because teeth often straightened out naturally from the pressure of the lips against them. Just as the dentist had predicted, my teeth did straighten without artificial help, and my parents were spared the ordeal and expense of orthodontia from their meager earnings. In those Depression years, it was highly unusual for people even to consider spending money on such an extravagance as straightening "a few crooked teeth." In matters concerning my health and welfare, my parents usually agreed.

Once because of Mother's limited English, I think I experienced a near-death episode. She misread the label on a bottle and gave me camphorated oil instead of castor oil for my constipation. After I ingested the dose, I felt wave after wave of strange ripples traveling through my body, and I lost all power of speech. I tried to call out to Mother, who was in the kitchen, but my vocal cords refused to cooperate. I remember thinking *Am I dying? Is this how it feels to die?* Then came an overwhelming nausea and I heaved up the camphorated oil, together with all my breakfast. With that I regained my speech and my "life."

Not everything about those days was bad. I had good times with Mother, and sometimes we all functioned harmoniously as a family. On some Saturdays Mother and I took the streetcar downtown to the Sumitomo Bank where she made her weekly deposit into the family savings account, then we shopped for fruits and vegetables at Pike Place Market. On our way home, she treated me to either lemon meringue pie or a 3-flavored ice cream cone—only five cents for three scoops!

Occasionally we went to the local movie theater in West Seattle to see American films that I translated for my mother in my "pigeon Japanese." Others in the theater were annoyed by our constant whispering and turned to glare or reprimand us. I, too, was irritated with Mother, for I could not fully enjoy the movie with her frequent interruptions. But on the whole, it was a peaceful time for the two of us, being away from Father.

When the weather was good Father usually went fishing, one activity he had enjoyed since his childhood. In those days Elliot Bay was clean and unpolluted, teeming with seafood, and as Father usually drank only at night, he never fell into the bay. He caught perch, rock cod, the small fish called "shiners," as well as shrimp and crab. To catch shrimp he dipped his net down against the barnacle-laden pier supports, bringing it up filled with small shrimp. He hung crab pots from the pier, tied them to the railing, and returned to check on them later. No one else touched his pots, for Dungeness crabs were plentiful enough for everyone. During salmon season he left the house when it was still dark and always came home with a good catch. Mother would slice up the salmon and send me off to distribute portions to our neighbors. She also marinated salmon steaks in *kasu* (rice wine lees). They were delicious fried or grilled; sometimes I got a bit tipsy after too much marinated steak.

When I was twelve I went with Father one day and caught a 12-pound fish—small for a salmon—but I was thrilled, although I needed Father's help to pull it in. He usually caught salmon in the 20-plus pound range, and once even a 34-pounder. In one of his rare moments of what might pass for affection, he took a picture of me proudly holding my catch. I think he was pleased that I had accompanied him; he was a very lonely man. That was the only time I went salmon fishing as a child—I was not a "morning person" and hated to get up before dawn just to catch fish.

An uneasy truce usually prevailed during family outings, and Father as a rule behaved well. We sometimes drove to beaches some distance from home. While Father dug for the large, obscene-looking geoduck clams with long fleshy necks that squirted water high into the air, Mother and I gathered seaweed that clung to rocks along the shore. At home she combined that seaweed with soy sauce, sugar and shiitake mushrooms to create *tsukudani*, a paste that we ate with hot rice. Butter-fried geoduck clams were chewy and tasty—one of my favorite shellfish.

In the fall we joined a group of neighbors and set forth to the Cascade Mountains for *matsutake tori* (pine mushroom-picking). These mushrooms, a great delicacy for the Japanese, grow only under red pine trees. They were so plentiful in season that Father usually picked almost a full gunnysack—perhaps as much as 100 pounds. Amateurs had difficulty finding them because most grew underground, but seasoned pickers could easily spot the dirt mounds that covered them. After removing a mushroom, the pickers carefully covered the hole so the spores remained intact for future growth. They had learned in Japan to treat nature with respect.

On the drive along the winding roads to the mountains, I invariably suffered from motion sickness and Father had to stop a few times. But I always recovered in time to enjoy the picnic lunches that Mother and the other women had prepared—different types of sushi, chicken tempura and various other treats. Most of the children were more interested in eating and playing in the woods than finding mushrooms. After our return, we shared our bounty with neighbors and friends. At home Mother added the mushrooms to our sukiyaki dinner or butter-fried a large frying pan full of mushrooms because that was one of my favorite dishes. (In the 1980s I would hear that pine mushrooms had become scarce and were selling for over $100 per 100 grams in Japan.)

Some Saturday nights we attended Japanese movies at *Nippon Kan* (Japan Hall) in town. My parents watched avidly, but I didn't understand much of the dialogue and only watched the flickering images until I fell asleep. Because I listened to Mother and her friends discuss the films, I still remember the names and faces of some of the famous movie stars of that era—Tanaka Kinuyo, Irie Takako, Uyehara Ken, Sano Shuji—. Those movies were mostly melodramas, with themes of lost love or of lovers forced to part by cruel circumstance.

In the summertime, the Issei from different prefectures in Japan held their own *Kenjin Kai* (Prefectural Association) picnics at Seward Park in Seattle. The ladies prepared huge amounts of food, and in addition to the Japanese fare, we children were offered barbecued hot dogs and soda pop. Since we ate mostly seafood at home, a hot dog was a great treat for me. The adults visited together, gossiping and catching up on the latest news. For the children, some of the fathers orchestrated various kinds of races—running with an egg on a spoon, three-legged contests, hopping in gunnysacks, and just plain foot races. Winners won small token prizes, such as pencils, crayons and Mickey Mouse tablets.

As most families did not have close relatives in America, they tended to treat others from the same prefecture (Japanese equivalent of U.S. state) like extended family. The first question often asked after introductions was: "What *ken* (prefecture) are you from?" If the other party happened to hail from the same place *and* near one's home village, he was treated almost like next of kin. Since my parents were from Yamaguchi Prefecture, their closest friends were also from Yamaguchi and our social life revolved around these people. One such friend was Mr. Nakamura, who owned the Atlas Hotel in the middle of Japan Town. And there, while the adults conversed, I watched a double-feature movie alone next door, amply supplied with popcorn and soda. My parents' oldest friends from logging camp days, the Teradas, also lived in Japan Town, and while the men reminisced about their work for the lumber company, Mrs. Terada and Mother discussed and exchanged books, for both possessed a literary bent. To be polite I played with the Teradas' son and daughter, both much younger than I.

I think Mrs. Yamasaki of the South Park section of Seattle was probably Mother's best friend, for Mother was at her most animated and smiling when she was with this friend. Mrs. Yamasaki had a lively personality, a quick sense of humor, and enough confidence to contradict her husband when she disagreed with him.

The two women co-workers enjoyed each other's company so much that we often visited the Yamasakis. Father did not object to these visits, so I suspect he also derived some pleasure in drinking and talking with Mr. Yamasaki.

The Yamasaki boys, Frank and Bob, were great teases. During dinner if I happened to look away, one of them would "steal" my drumstick and I'd spot it on one of their plates. While the adults talked shop and shared memories of their homeland, I spent time playing games with Frank, three years older than I, whose personality was much like his mother's. We got along well and he even tried to train a pigeon to fly messages to my home. The bird never did learn. On the other hand, Bob usually ignored me after dinner because he was busy with his studies. One day, however, when I was about eleven, Bob spoke to me seriously, or so I thought. He said, "I'll take you out to a dance when you turn 16, but first you must pluck your eyebrows (mine were thick and wide) and make yourself look pretty." My immediate reaction to the thought of going out with a boy several years older was thrilling, and I could hardly wait to grow up. But on reflection I wasn't so sure his remarks added up to a compliment. In my young life the Yamasaki boys filled the role of cousins I never knew.

On the occasions when Father drank too much during our visits, Mother took over as chauffeur. She was a hyper-nervous driver, who never did learn how to use a clutch properly. So anxious was she that she once pulled up to a gas station and backed right up into a gas pump. It's a wonder she did not start a fire. I'm not sure which was worse for me, Father's erratic driving under the influence or Mother's edgy, jerky performance behind the wheel. It amazes me how I managed to survive the hazards of being an only child in that family.

11

FUN TIMES

When I look back on my adventurous and bountiful childhood among friends in West Seattle, I am filled with nostalgia. Mother and I both loved the beautiful setting of West Seattle. Wild trilliums and delicate dogwood graced the woods in springtime, and in summer tiger lilies lit up the hillside. The Japanese culinary delicacy bracken abounded, and watercress flourished beside a stream at the foot of the hill. Golden scotch broom brightened the roadsides. Mother and most of our neighbors loved to garden, and flowers and vegetable gardens surrounded almost all of the old houses. Mother planted myriad roses, irises, hydrangeas and gladioli in addition to her favorite daffodils. And the fresh, clean fragrance of lilacs outside my bedroom window after a spring rain intoxicated me.

Some Japanese families in West Seattle constructed their own baths like those back home; Father eventually added one adjacent to our house. But before that, we and a few other families shared a communal *ofuro* (Japanese bath) built by Mr. Ishii, for even in this tiny outpost on foreign soil, the Issei created that all-important touch of Japan. I recall how my mother scrubbed and rinsed my back before I held my breath and slowly submerged in what felt almost like boiling water and nestled on her lap while the steam rose around us. I recall how she sighed contentedly and chatted with friends. Bath time was a peaceful, friendly, homey time for the families. Masako, nicknamed Massi, the Ishii daughter who shared these experiences, once told me that my mother occasionally lined up all the children in the bathhouse and taught us songs. I have no recollection of this, but such behavior would be very much in character for one who had once aspired to become a teacher.

In preparation for New Year's Day, the community came together for *mochi tsuki* (pounding rice cake). For this treat the women cooked mounds of sweet, sticky rice that the men pounded in large receptacles with wooden mallets. Some of the women took turns stirring the hot rice with hands dipped in cold water for each stir. The men intoned a rhythmic chant, coordinating their pounding with the ladies' stirring. Other women carried the finished product to a huge table in the Ishii home, where they quickly tore off bits, rolling them into small balls and flattening them down to small rounds. Sweet bean paste was inserted into some of the rice balls—all of which were called *mochi.* A traditional New Year's celebration without *mochi* was unthinkable for we all started each year with a breakfast of *ozoni*, mochi soup. We also toasted mochi and flavored it in a dip of soy sauce and sugar. Our parents told us children that we should eat as many rice cakes as our age–a more difficult task than it might appear, for even a few mochi lay heavily on the stomach.

For days Mother and other women prepared other traditional dishes for New Year's Day, when their festive offerings and *sake* (rice wine) were served to all guests. At the center of the laden table sat either a whole broiled red sea bream or red snapper with its tail curled, symbolizing the auspiciousness of the occasion. A dish of black beans was included to represent health for the coming year.

A variety of the other dishes also signified good fortune or health. This was the only time of year that Mother purchased imported tangerines individually wrapped in paper. The women remained in their own homes all day to serve guests, while the men made the rounds of all their neighbors and close friends inside and outside the community to make their New Year's salutations.

We children also looked forward to New Year's because it was on that day that we received our presents, not on Christmas. Our parents bought gifts, not only for their own children but also for others in the community—either inexpensive toys or clothes and other useful items. We youngsters were pleased with whatever we received, for our expectations were not high.

During the summer months we children had countless adventures in the woods behind our homes and on Elliot Bay. We were unsupervised, for our erstwhile babysitter, Massi's mother, now worked outside the home since her youngest was no longer a toddler. Left on our own, we learned to be independent and resourceful. Our parents did not worry that strangers might harm us because child predators were unheard of. We picked wild salmonberries, blackberries and hazel nuts in the woods, and also climbed trees and built tree houses. One of our favorite haunts was our very own swimming hole, a small cove on Elliot Bay down the hill from our homes, where someone had built a two-tiered diving board. Massi, the neighborhood boys, and I were all self-taught swimmers and divers. Massi could swim long distances, but I was not a strong swimmer so I worked on my diving skills. It took some time before I screwed up enough courage to climb up onto the high board. The water was so cold that we built bonfires before taking our dips, warming ourselves by the fireside when we came out of the water covered with goose bumps, shivering from the cold. When we could we pooled our money for marshmallows to toast; at other times we roasted potatoes in the ashes. Seattle summers were so cool that we always waited until the temperature rose to at least 70 degrees Fahrenheit before we thought it warm enough to swim.

When the tide went out, we waded barefoot in the shallow channels. Once I felt something slippery under my foot and reached down and pulled up a flounder. I had caught a fish with my bare hands! Mother cooked it that night and, because it was my own catch, I thought it was the most delicious fish ever.

Massi, a pretty, muscular girl two years my senior, and I were the tomboys of the neighborhood. We played with the boys and tested our mettle by doing what they did. In fact, Massi was so "rough and tough" she could beat up any boy who annoyed her— or me. She appointed herself my protector and challenged those who teased me or denigrated me in any way. She also ordered me around, and I usually listened to her because I knew that under her rough exterior, she was a good-hearted soul. As most of the families kept rowboats tied to a landing at the base of the hill, we children took to rowing our boats far out on Elliot Bay and often racing each other. Massi was the strongest rower, but I held my own: I often out-rowed some of the boys.

We also fished from the pier and, like Father, caught perch, rock cod, and shiners. We tossed away ling cod, which were inedible. Massi taught me how to bait a fishhook and remove a fish from it. Mother cleaned the shiners, pickled them in vinegar and sugar, and we ate them head and all.

Intrepid Massi and I once had a harrowing experience on an excursion to harvest shrimp. We were so engrossed in netting our catch that we did not realize we had drifted too close to the support posts of a train trestle that ran across the pier. Before we knew it, our boat was wedged so tightly between the posts that we could not move at all. With the tide coming in, I thought our boat would be flooded and we'd have to swim to shore. But twelve-year-old Massi sprang into action. She ordered me to sit on one side of the boat so it tipped a little and she began gently rocking it. Then she pushed against one of the posts with an oar, and we were freed. I sighed with relief, and my admiration for my dauntless friend knew no bounds.

In view of her customary brashness, most people were surprised whenever Massi showed her softer side. She could play by ear on the organ any tune she heard without ever taking a lesson. She played with two hands, chords and all. I can still hear her in my head, playing "Harbor Lights" and other popular tunes. I was particularly impressed because Mother had allowed me to take piano lessons from one of the nuns at school, but I was so clumsy I simply could not make my hands play different notes at the same time. I soon gave up the effort.

Now and then a Japanese freighter docked at a pier about a mile from our community. The merchant marines welcomed us aboard, allowed us to explore their ship, and even gave us gifts from Japan. When I was still quite small, the men picked me up and gave me rides on their shoulders. My parents and neighbors feted the sea-weary men with sumptuous dinners. Those were exciting highlights in our lives.

One of my fondest memories is of sleepovers with another favorite friend, Anne Nakamura, a classmate from Maryknoll Elementary School. As our parents came from neighboring villages in Japan, we were almost like kin. Father did not drink much or act out during Anne's visits, for which I was most grateful. My mother introduced her to fresh crab, shrimp and fish, which Anne thought delicious. Inasmuch as she lived in town, her family did not have access to seafood straight out of the water as we did. And she also found our *ofuro* an intriguing change from her own tub at home. I took her to visit Massi and other friends in the neighborhood, and I think her weekend stays at my home might have been mini-vacations for her because, as the only daughter, she had many chores assigned to her at home. Staying at her place on Beacon Hill was a lively change for me, too, as she had three brothers and I enjoyed feeling part of a larger family.

Although our parents actively tried to discourage us from playing with neighborhood white children, we youngsters were not color conscious and for the most part ignored their admonitions. A good-natured, redheaded Irish boy whom we called Carrot-top loved to join our softball games in the clearing adjacent to the Ishii home. Seattle is so far north that in summer it is light until late at night, and we often played outdoors until about 9:00 or 10:00 p.m. before our parents called us home.

Our families never took vacations. The closest I ever came to anything like a vacation was one week's stay at a truck farm owned by family friends. When I arrived alone carrying my little suitcase, the lady of the house, Mrs. Uyegaki, was amazed that a 10-year-old could travel alone by streetcar and bus to arrive safely at their farm. It was only a distance of perhaps seven miles, and I was accustomed to exploring by myself. The Uyegaki's daughter, Sachiko, and I ran all over the farm, fed the horses, pestered the farm hands, and in general, made nuisances of ourselves. But Sachiko's parents were loving, lenient people and did not scold us. They seemed pleased to have a playmate for their only child. Compared to plump Sachiko, I looked much like a scarecrow, and Mrs. Uyegaki took it upon herself to fatten me up. She fed me and fed me. "Eat! Eat!" she'd say, "You need to put meat on your bones." And I did my best to fill myself with the chicken, fresh corn, beets and other bounty she placed before me. I had never eaten fresh beets before, and those she had just pulled up from her garden tasted divinely sweet. To this day, whenever I have fresh beets I think fondly of Mrs. Uyegaki.

In 1937, when Massi completed seventh grade, she and her two brothers were sent to Hiroshima City in Japan to live with their aunt and attend Japanese schools. I missed her dearly, for she had been my favorite companion in our many adventures, and I saw no choice but to spend more time with other acquaintances in the neighborhood. Since I had little in common with the other two older Nisei girls in our community, I chose to spend time with Caucasian girls living nearby. I played Chinese checkers and Monopoly with Theda, whose mother kept dozens of canaries. (Her stagestruck mother had named Theda after the silent film actress Theda Bara.) An overprotected child, she had a sweet disposition and always welcomed me when I turned up at her door. However, at times the combined odors of bird dung and urine-soaked clothing (Theda was plagued by enuresis) sickened me and I left early. She seldom, if ever, left home on her own. In contrast, golden-haired June was more action-oriented. She and I roller-skated, played on a boat landing near her home, and went to the movies together. Her Swedish mother often invited me to lunch at their home and was always kind and friendly.

Off and on I visited with Alice Anderson, a woman in her twenties who was in an advanced stage of muscular dystrophy. Her mother had died some years before, and Alice lived in a little brick house with her father and brother. By the time I met her, Alice walked with crutches, drooled a lot, and spoke with difficulty. Yet she somehow managed to look after herself while the men folk worked. She welcomed any sort of company, and I remember balancing my way across the top of a towering billboard to entertain her, while she "Ooh'd" and "Aah'd." I was sure-footed and fearless and did not think of the possible consequences of my feat. If Mother had seen me in action, she would have had a panic attack.

Some days I spent hours alone at home reading. When I tired of my solitude I hopped on the streetcar and visited friends in the city. During the summer months the streetcar fare was only two cents for children with no additional charge for transfers, and I made good use of the bargain. I visited Yasuko Kubo, whose parents owned a hotel where I loved to pump out tunes on the player piano, songs such as "Pagan Love Song" and "Just a Song at Twilight." Anne Nakamura and I went to Mt. Baker Bathing Beach on

Lake Washington, where there were lifeguards and a raft one could swim to and dive from. The lake water was much warmer than our swimming hole on the bay, but it took more effort to float in fresh water than in salt water. I wasn't sure which I preferred.

In the summer right after I graduated from Maryknoll, in 1940, I joined a group of Nisei friends to work at the Shigiyo Farm, about 15 miles from home. The farm had separate dormitories for girls and boys, as well as a communal Japanese-style bathhouse we all shared. This was the closest any of us came to "camping." Our parents came to visit us on weekends and helped us pick berries. Most of us were saving our pay to buy school clothes and other necessities. During the day we picked raspberries or strawberries, then after dinner and bath, we walked down to the White River to cool off and skip stones over the water. Anne, an athletic girl, always did well in these contests. I enjoyed those days of companionship with a large group of other young people.

Grace Uyehara, Anne Nakamura, Jean and Mother at Farm

Although summers were fun and filled with easy entertainment, the winter months with their dreary gray skies and almost cease-less rain made me lonely. I didn't relish going home after school to an empty house, so I often stopped by to see our neighbor, Hatsu Iwago. She was a stay-at-home mother in her twenties with one daughter. Her husband owned a gasoline station near Japan Town and did not come home until late, so she was pleased to have my company. She treated me to snacks and homemade root beer, taught me how to sew, and played cards with me. At Mother's request, it was Hatsu who taught me the "facts of life." Her sex education consisted of giving me a book to read about the biologi-cal differences between men and women and how babies are born. That was it!

Decades have passed since I left my childhood home in West Seattle, but I still recall with pleasure the times I shared with my friends. And although the site of the old Japanese settlement is now covered over with condominiums, that special community lives on in my memory.

12

"NO JAPS ALLOWED"

On the surface my social life seemed serene, but from time to time I felt the sting of prejudice. The "No Japs Allowed" signs posted at the Alki swimming pool troubled me deeply, for I loved to swim and longed to test my skills in the pool. *Do they consider me unclean?* I wondered. That seemed ironic because most Japanese bathed daily, whereas many of our white friends took baths only on Saturday night. But I knew deep down that cleanliness was not the real issue. Nor was I oblivious to the name-calling and the times I was deliberately ignored or kept waiting needlessly by salespeople at the Kress's five-and-dime store and at Rhodes Department Store. All this made me vow that some day I would show them "I'm just as good as you."

Beneath the surface I was torn between two worlds—two cultures. Even at school we saluted the flag and spoke only English outside of the Japanese class. Few of us took it seriously in any case, because a part of us wanted to reject the culture that was so scorned by the mainstream. I watched Hollywood movies and listened to popular music and soap operas on the radio. I ate hot dogs and hamburgers at picnics and played with my white friends, June and Theda. I wanted to blend in and be accepted. And I thought to be accepted, I must be more like the whites.

At home I spoke a halting Japanese with my parents and listened to their conversations about the Sino-Japanese war and of the various injustices they had experienced. I learned Japanese values and traditions by listening to my mother and observing her behavior. I learned the virtues of *gaman* (endurance), *gambare* (perseverance), *orei* (return of gifts and favors), *koden* (funeral money gifts), *on* (obligation) or *giri* (duty), and *ninjo* (compassion). I learned it was supremely important to keep a balanced ledger in the areas of *orei* and *koden*: the Issei in fact kept actual ledgers noting the names and amounts they gave or were given as *koden* so that they could reciprocate in kind when necessary. As for *orei*, if we gave salmon or crabs to our neighbors, they invariably reciprocated with some sort of vegetable from their gardens or some other homemade or homegrown gift. No matter how busy or tired Mother was, she found time to pay calls, to accord her respects wherever due.

One of the stronger Japanese means of control was the persistent question, "What will people think?" My mother repeated this phrase over and over in her attempts to get me to conform to her standards of behavior. I also sensed, in my parents' derogatory remarks about the whites and their admonitions to avoid the "wild ways" of the white kids, *and* in their praise of Japanese virtues, a strong "us-versus-them" mentality. Too, I noted mixed feelings of inferiority and superiority—superiority in their cultural pride and inferiority in their economic status and relative lack of power.

As anti-Japanese sentiments in the United States grew in the late 1930s, my parents talked increasingly of returning to Japan. Mrs. Yamasaki told Mother that her son, Frank, had been attacked when he was delivering newspapers. Other such incidents against the Japanese were on the rise. (I also suspect that Father, who had immigrated illegally, feared that authorities might soon question his status.) Then, in 1940, sensing the imminent outbreak of the war, my parents finally made their move.

I had just entered my freshman year at West Seattle High School, where I was the only Japanese-American in the class. A large number of Nisei attended Broadway High School, which was close to downtown Seattle, and I could have gone there, too. But with the knowledge that we would leave in November, it seemed pointless for me to commute that distance for such a short period of time. I would immediately regret my choice, however, because at West Seattle High I would experience discrimination from a teacher for the first time in my academic life. Although I had always excelled in my studies at Maryknoll Elementary, my high school algebra teacher, a dour-faced older woman, gave me my first "C." I was certain I had done the work correctly, but I knew intuitively that she disliked me and would not hear me out if I tried to question her. Only one girl made friendly overtures to me, and the others either ignored or ostracized me.

Soon I began to develop various psychosomatic symptoms—headaches and stomachaches—from the stress of the social isolation. About nine weeks into the school year, without my parents' knowledge or permission, I signed myself out of school, telling the principal that our family was moving to Japan and I could no longer attend. Thus I extricated myself from an intolerable situation and gave myself a two-week vacation before we left. My parents never did find out that I spent that time attending movies and visiting Hatsu Iwago, our neigbor, who I swore to secrecy.

When the time actually came for us to leave, I could not believe it. I had so looked forward to my high school years: the parties, dancing, dating and pretty clothes. Maybe at the other high school, I thought ruefully, all that would have become reality. Besides, some Nisei friends who had visited and returned from Japan talked of the constricted lifestyle there, especially for women.

"I don't want to go, Mama," I announced on the eve of our departure.

"You have to go. You belong with your parents." Then her voice softened as she noticed my anxiety. "We'll be a whole family again." Her words rang hollow as I thought of the friends and dreams I must leave behind.

On November 28, 1940 my parents and I sailed from Seattle Harbor on the *Hikawa Maru*. It was a bleak, overcast day, reflecting my own mood. Colorful streamers, blaring music and tearful farewells evoked memories of the day my brothers had left. Four friends came to see me off, and I half-heartedly tossed a few streamers down to them and forced myself to smile. As I watched the shoreline of my homeland——the land of my birth—recede into the misty distance, I wondered whether I would ever see my friends again. Would I ever come home again?

Four friends, Yuriko, Anne, Aya and Chieko, see me off at
Seattle Wharf

III.

LIFE IN WARTIME JAPAN

13

CULTURE SHOCK

Miracles do happen, I thought. As soon as we boarded the ship, Father stopped drinking! Perhaps it was living in close quarters with so many others that inhibited him, or perhaps some other impulse was at work. Whatever the motive, he quit alcohol cold turkey. Needless to say, Mother and I were immensely pleased to be spared the anxiety and embarrassment caused by his drunken behavior. Without the drink, his whole demeanor changed; he became strangely subdued, confused, lost—almost shy. I felt rather sorry for him.

The ship made an overnight stop in Vancouver, British Columbia, where a contingent of Canadian Nisei came on board, on their way to see relatives in Japan. I would spend most of the voyage visiting and enjoying shipboard activities with them. One girl, Nancy Kido, and I walked the decks together, played cards with "the boys" and sometimes danced with them. This contact with new friends turned out to be a pleasant hiatus for me between life in America and the unknown awaiting us in Japan. The ship's crew spoke little

English, and I soon realized I really could not carry on a decent conversation in Japanese. How would I fare in Japan with such limitations?

From Vancouver the ship headed into the Northern Pacific, and as we sailed past the Aleutians we saw whales swimming at a distance, spouting now and then. The ship creaked and groaned during storms until I feared it might split in two. I had heard of that actually happening to vessels and envisioned an end in icy waters. But after fourteen days on heaving seas, we finally came safely in sight of Japan.

Jean on Hikawa Maru, 1940

"There's land! I see Japan!" a man shouted with joy.

Passengers poured on deck. For some Issei it was the first glimpse of home in decades; for young Nisei like myself it was the introduction to the "old country" of our parents. As we drew into Yokohama Harbor, scattered Western-style buildings, myriad tile-roofed homes, crooked streets, trees, then people gradually took shape. Mt. Fuji rose majestically above the clouds in the distance, just like the picture on our calendar.

Mother turned to me and said in a little-girl voice, "Look, Yasue. Look. Japan. We've finally come home."

Home? I thought. *This is not my home.*

Father, as was usual for him on emotional occasions, stood by silently. I wasn't sure whether I should feel excited or frightened. My own conversational ability here would be less than adequate. On the other hand, I looked forward to meeting my sisters and other relatives at last, and seeing my brothers again.

We stayed over the first night at a Yokohama inn, and in the morning took a train to a small town in Shizuoka Prefecture, then transferred to a bus that carried us up into the mountains to a reform school where my brother, Frank Tsutomu, had been sent for "delinquent" behavior. Frank was overjoyed to see us, for I'm sure he thought we had come to rescue him forthwith. The head of the reformatory extolled Frank's virtues—good nature, kindness and intelligence—and said candidly that Frank did not belong there. The boy would be released to his grandparents' home for New Year's and we could meet him there at that time.

After saying goodbye to a somewhat crestfallen Frank, we caught another train to Wakamatsu City in Fukuoka Prefecture, where my two sisters had been living for 18 years with our maternal grand-parents. I could hardly contain my excitement as we approached our destination. It was an eerie sensation to be meeting my sisters for the first time at age 14. Both were smaller than I: Misae Rose, at 19, was about five feet tall; and Shizue May, 18, about three inches shorter. I was already nearly half a foot taller than Shizue May and still had another inch or so to grow! They both wore kimono, and we all eyed each other curiously. Misae Rose, the elder of the two and the family extrovert, made friendly overtures, trying to engage me in conversation. I could understand most of what she said, but hadn't the vocabulary to respond intelligently. Shizue May, the quiet one, watched me closely but spoke hardly a word. Both of them were veritable strangers to me, for not only had we never met but we had no common upbringing. They had been steeped in Japanese culture and tradition, whereas I was accustomed to a kind of freedom they knew nothing about.

My brothers also joined us in Wakamatsu at New Year's, Frank from Shizuoka Prefecture and John from Yanai, Yamaguchi Prefecture, where he now attended high school and boarded in the home of Uncle Hamaguchi and his wife. My grandparents had found dealing with the two boys taxing after John and Frank reached their teenage years and shifted the responsibility for their discipline to Uncle Hamaguchi, whose stern hand, they thought, would keep them in line. And it was Uncle Hamaguchi who had sent Frank to the reformatory, after consulting with his wife and our grandparents. Frank later confided to me that when Mother received a letter from our relatives asking how they should deal with him, she simply told them to do whatever was best for the family. Frank never forgave Mother for that.

Almost eight years had elapsed since my brothers and I had seen each another, and they responded to me in different ways. Frank chattered happily, as if we had parted only yesterday. John cast a few furtive looks at us, followed by only tentative overtures. It was an awkward and poignant time for me, for I did not know quite what to do or say to them. Even so, I felt strongly bonded to both, for we three had suffered much together at Father's hand as small children.

All my siblings seemed a bit jealous of me and considered me the favored child because I was the only one of us that our parents had raised from birth. Of course they had no idea of my trials as the only child back home. Misae Rose showed that she thought it fun to have another sister, especially one brought up in America, as she was outgoing and curious about life outside Japan. And, too, she could afford to be magnanimous because our grandmother doted on her. Frank, the family scapegoat, saw me as an ally and was pleased that I had joined the family. Shizue May and John remained standoffish. I think John felt I had usurped his privileged position as the youngest in the family, and although Grandmother treated him with special care, he knew he was not her favorite. Shizue May stayed in the background and did not interact much with anyone, so far as I could tell.

Not long after our initial welcome, by the end of December, tensions started to build in the home. This was not due to Father, I hasten to say, for he continued his abstinence and created no scenes. I suspect my parents had made no real plans when they left America, perhaps hoping to live indefinitely with our grandparents. Certainly Mother had sent her parents a goodly sum of money through the years—enough for them to rebuild their business so that they were prosperous once again—and Grandfather Nakamoto remained friendly and kind. But Grandmother became more and more distant and made it increasingly clear that we were in the way. Always penurious, she appeared to have forgotten that her daughter had sacrificed herself in marriage in order to save the Nakamoto family. There would be no reciprocation now when her own daughter needed help. I don't know how Mother felt about this situation for she remained silent, but I noticed she seemed unhappy and at loose ends.

Immediately after the New Year holidays, we moved to Aunt and Uncle Hamaguchi's home in the town of Yanai. At the same time Frank started work at a factory in the nearby town of Hikari and came to visit us. Only the youngest Hamaguchi daughter, Kimie, a high school senior, remained at home with her parents. Thus three members of the Hamaguchi family and four of ours, including John, lived together for three months.

Frank Tsutomu (16) 1941

Mother had tried to get me through the back door into academic high schools in both Fukuoka and Yamaguchi Prefectures, but no school would accept me because of my inadequate command of the language. I refused to attend a domestic arts high school, and I couldn't understand why my parents would not enroll me in the mission high school in Hiroshima City. It accepted Nisei students with language limitations, and my childhood friend Massi was a student there. Perhaps they still needed me as a buffer, for even though Father had stopped drinking they had little to say to each other. Had I attended the school in Hiroshima City, I would probably have died in the A-bomb blast.

In any case, Mother enrolled me in January in Yanai Elementary School, where I was placed in *fifth grade*. To be demoted four grades in school was a devastating blow to the ego of a teenager who had always been a top student in America. I was taller than average to begin with, and being put back with younger, much smaller students made me stand out all the more. Mr. Yasui, our teacher, was sensitive to my unhappy position, and told me I need not remove my blouse for *kampu masatsu* (dry towel massage) in which all students removed their upper garments and rubbed themselves with towels. An essentially kind man, he also tried to ease my school experience in other ways.

Jean in School Uniform, 1941

During our initial days in Yanai, I clung to Mother and felt insecure whenever she was out of sight, for she was my translator and intermediary in this hostile new world. I had been such an independent child until then, but the unexpected stresses reduced me to toddler-like behavior. When we went shopping, for instance, I remained close to her for fear of separation, because without her I might not be able to find my way home or ask for directions. At night I had frightful dreams of being stranded and alone in a strange place.

Mother, through no fault of her own, lacked the understanding to help me deal with my culture shock. Because both she and Father had left Japan as teenagers they, too, were experiencing difficulties adjusting to life as adults in their homeland. Thus I faced life in a newly cold and merciless, militaristic Japan without a single close ally. In this environment, my gregarious tomboy days ended and my isolation took root. It was a time of anti-American slogans, and anything American was suspect. I was ignored, stared at, followed, and called "Yankee girl." Even my relatives and siblings, especially John, treated me as if I were somewhat retarded. Only Cousin Kimie behaved in a warm manner toward me. Being "different" in Japan was anathema. I was overwhelmed by the abrupt lifestyle change and felt a helpless rage.

Just around that time Massi, my childhood friend, came to visit me in Yanai. Since coming to Japan she had learned that her own father had died early and that Mr. Ishii, who had raised her, was actually her stepfather. Her father, a Mr. Nosho, had owned a lumberyard and sawmill in Japan, and Massi found herself an heiress to a small fortune. She had come to rescue me. "Why don't you run away with me? she urged. "I have plenty of money, and I'll buy our tickets and we'll go back to Seattle together. I'll take care of you. But we'd better hurry while there are still ships leaving for the States." What a tempting offer that was! I could leave behind this horrible nightmare of my life in Japan and be free again! But thoughts of Mother's probable reactions—sadness, loneliness and bewilderment—held me back, and very reluctantly I refused the offer. In any case, neither Massi nor I realized that without a passport and an adult vouching for me in America, I probably would not have been allowed to board any ship. Massi, however, did manage to leave Japan on the last ship.

During my early months in Japan I often thought about an essay entitled "Conflict" I had read in America. The Nisei writer felt she was "neither fish nor fowl"—part of neither the American culture nor of the Japanese. That is exactly how I felt. In America I had been called "Jap" and told to "go back home," and here in Japan I was called "Yankee girl" and treated like a pariah. In the land where everyone had black hair, I had thought I would be accepted, but I was wrong. Where *did* I belong? Was there no place for me?

Living in our relatives' home did not work out. My parents said nothing, but I could sense that they found the parsimonious ways of Aunt and Uncle Hamaguchi hard to tolerate. After the school year ended in March (the Japanese school year begins in April and ends in March of the following year), Father and I traveled to Suo Oshima Island in Yamaguchi Prefecture, my parents' birthplace, to consult with one of his uncles about finding a home in their village. Through the uncle's help, Father learned of a house to rent in Amafuri, the hamlet where Mother was born. The house still belonged to one of Mother's relatives who had emigrated to Hawaii and established a department store. My parents then settled on Suo Oshima Island, known for its temperate climate and idyllic setting on the Seto Inland Sea. They were home at last. My siblings all insisted on remaining where they were, so I again became an only child. Since both of my parents had grown up on Suo Oshima Island and Mother was part of the well-known Nakamoto family, friends and relatives greeted their return warmly. As I was part of both the Nakamoto and Oda clans, I was no longer treated as badly as I had been in Yanai; I was accepted because I was one of them—not an outsider— despite my funny accent. Mother enrolled me in the local elementary school in the sixth grade in April. Here again I stood out as the tallest in the class, but the students were not as cruel as at the other school. I walked about half a mile to and from school with other children from the hamlet.

Father was in his glory! He went fishing almost daily and brought home sea bream, eel, tuna or squid. On the days he did not fish, a fishmonger came to sell us fresh seafood from wooden buckets balanced on his shoulders. Mother worked in her vegetable garden, gathered *wakame* and *hijiki* seaweed, sea urchins and oysters. Neighbors, friends, and relatives stopped by to chat or bring us vegetables or sweet potatoes. Life in Amafuri hamlet was bountiful and peaceful; my parents seemed to be content for the first time.

14

PEARL HARBOR DAY IN JAPAN

In contrast to the shock, anger and mourning in America on what President Roosevelt called "a date which will live in infamy," the Pearl Harbor attack was greeted with wild enthusiasm all over Japan. The airwaves hummed with excitement, while newspaper headlines heralded the event with jubilation. "Our Imperial navy and air force have demolished the mighty giant's navy" was the recurring theme of the day.

I heard the news at our morning assembly at school on December 8, 1941[6] when our principal announced dramatically, "We are at war with America." Oh, no, I thought, I'm stuck here in Japan for good. I was shocked that my country and my parents' country were fighting each other; and as a fifteen-year-old, my initial reactions of course centered entirely on my own situation and how this war would affect me.

The principal continued with a further assertion that would be oft-repeated in the days and weeks to come: "As we all know, our

---

6 Because of the International Date Line, Pearl Harbor Day was a day later in Japan than in the United States.

enemies have encircled Japan with the ABCD Line—America, Britain, China and the Dutch—and we had no recourse but to defend ourselves. In addition, Roosevelt [has] placed an embargo against Japan that deprives us of resources essential to our survival. As we all know, we have very few natural resources in our country, and with [the Americans'] sanctions, they hoped to strangle us economically. Before they attacked us, we had to take the initiative." He then spoke at length about the many injustices perpetrated against Japan by the United States and its allies, and of the Western imperialists' desire to control all of Asia: "They could not abide Japan's military successes in China." This is how he explained not only the surprise attack on Pearl Harbor but also Japan's invasion of Manchuria and China.

We later learned that what the principal had to say about the rationale behind the U.S. embargo against Japan was not mere propaganda. Many historians subsequently claimed that Roosevelt did in fact provoke the attack with the embargoes on oil, scrap iron and other commodities in an acknowledged effort to stop Japan's expansion in Asia. Further, Roosevelt was known to favor U.S. entry into the European War against Hitler, partly to assist his European allies, but also to stimulate a domestic economy still crippled by more than a decade in the Great Depression. There also is evidence that the President knew in advance of the impending attack on Pearl Harbor but did nothing to stop it because he knew it would force U.S. entry into a conflict that inevitably would encompass Germany as well as Japan and hence compel the support of both the Congress and the U.S. citizenry in the European conflict. For Roosevelt, the Pearl Harbor attack probably felt Heaven-sent.

At school in Japan, the older boys now were trained to fight with wooden rifles, while the girls learned *naginata* (a Japanese women's martial art that makes use of long poles with pointed ends). The country wanted a strong, healthy population, and right after morning assembly we did about half an hour of calisthenics, plus another hour during the day of physical education. Mandatory annual physical endurance tests assessed the students' physical strength—timed running of 1,000 meters, jump-roping 500 times, crossing the parallel bars for as many times as we could, and turning over head first, then feet first on horizontal bars. I was able to manage most of the tests but never mastered turning over feet first on the horizontal bar.

As Japan's supply of imported scrap metals neared exhaustion, the government ordered citizens to contribute all their extra metal possessions, including pots and pans and even jewelry, for the war effort. Mother hid her jewelry—diamond and pearl pendants and a sapphire ring—because she wanted to save it for me; Father hid his large gold nugget, a souvenir from the Alaska adventure. To our surprise, government officials even confiscated Father's shortwave radio, although no one had accused him of spying. Mother warned me: "Don't say anything good about America or anything bad about Japan, or else you might get into trouble."

The Japanese military went on to invade much of Asia and the South Sea Islands—Hong Kong, Singapore, French Indo-China, Malaysia, Indonesia, the Philippines, Guam, Wake and other islands. With each conquest the Japanese population exulted. More and more young men were drafted into military service, and often the woman who feared she would end up an "old maid" married the first man available before he was sent to the front. Mothers, wives and children waved flags and shouted, "Banzai! Banzai!"[7] as their men left to go to war. No one dared show misgivings but what mother or wife or child could be happy when a loved one faced death, injury or illness in some foreign land.

Patriotic songs were ubiquitous—on the radio, at school and in the shops. *The Naval Song of the Great Asian War*[8] was heard constantly:

---

7 "Banzai" literally means ten thousand years, or "May the Emperor live ten thousand years," or used for "hurrah!"
8 Lyrics by Shintaro Kato, Music by Kunihiko Hashimoto.

Look at our glorious naval flag
Fluttering high above on the mast
When the time came, at a single command
On the morning of December 8th
First the stars and stripes torn asunder
Great battleships ripped, then sunk.

On that day the brave sons of the heroes
Who gave their lives at Lyunshun[9]
Dove down into Pearl Harbor.
Oh, how our hundred million mourned
The five submarines and nine heroes[10]
who failed to return,
Blown to bits by bombs, now enshrined as Gods of War.

The song continued for three more verses, extolling the bravery of Japanese naval forces in the South Seas, the Coral Sea and the Indian Ocean.

Since military needs were given priority, civilian food was rationed and we found ourselves eating more barley and sweet potatoes. On Suo Oshima Island we were fortunate that fresh seafood was plentiful and citrus fruit grew in abundance. For want of a good shampoo, Mother washed my hair with *funori*, a type of seaweed, which left my hair clean and glossy. She also cooked *kombu* (kelp) in various dishes, claiming that it would turn my brownish hair jet-black, the standard for beautiful hair. When the only doctor in the village failed to cure my affliction of boils, she resorted to folk medicine. She picked *niwatoko* (elder tree leaves), moistened

---

9 Lynshun, Manchuria was a naval base near Dairen during the Russo-Japanese War.

10 Two men manned each of the five small submarines lost in the attack, and the sole survivor was never officially recognized for his heroism by the Japanese government.

them and applied them directly to the lesions. The herbs drew the infection from the boils, and I was healed.

As a sentimental adolescent, I sometimes gazed at the moon and wondered what friends in the States were doing. Were they having fun? What was I missing? Did they remember me? Years later I learned that all those of Japanese ancestry living on the West Coast of the United States—including most of my friends—had been incarcerated in what were euphemistically called "relocation camps" in desolate desert areas.

At that time the Japanese school system was based on the German model: six years of elementary school and four years of high school. Those who did not go on to high school attended *Koto-ka*, a mandatory two additional years of low-level academic studies. Prefectural and private high schools required students to pass entrance examinations and their courses were on a higher level. Once I mastered the language I did well in all my classes, for they covered material I had already learned. The principal allowed me to skip one year, from sixth grade to the second year of Koto-ka, where I no longer stood out because of my height; indeed, a few other students were just as tall. Even so, I was still two years older than most of my classmates, who had started school a year later than those in America. My increased ability to express myself in Japanese by then had improved to the extent that some of the other students copied my test papers.

Mr. Kawai, our teacher at Koto-ka was different from the other faculty in that he never spouted wartime slogans or propaganda. Instead, he taught us "meditation," asking us to close our eyes, try to clear our minds and think of nothing. *Muga* (selflessness), he called it. We students were not aware that he was teaching us Zen meditation. I'm sure it took more than a little courage to be a pacifist in wartime Japan. To encounter such a gentle, centered man in this setting gave me hope that life could be good again some day. (Years later I wrote to him, telling him that his example had led me to see "the light at the end of the [war] tunnel.") My letter pleased him. He told Mother during a parent-teacher conference that I was an outstanding student and did not belong in this school. I did not take this as a compliment, for I knew I was merely reviewing in another language material I had already learned in English, and I was still two to three years behind my peers in America.

Mother had taken me to Kuka Prefectural Girls' High School several miles from our home to see if they would allow me to enroll. Officials there had told Mother I could return to take a high school transfer test for the third year after I completed my second year at Koto-ka. Later, however, they rescinded their promise and Mother accepted the decision without protest. I was furious and felt so betrayed that I swore I would master Japanese better than the native-born and show them how wrong they were.[11]

In hindsight I must say it was just as well that I wasn't accepted at the prefectural school because about then I became ill. I began spiking a fever every afternoon and grew disturbingly listless. Mother then took me to Yanai on Honshu Island, where more medical specialists were available. There, the doctor in charge diagnosed a light case of tuberculosis. I had just graduated from Koto-ka and was wondering what to do next when, to my great surprise, my parents informed me we were moving to Osaka. Were they bored with the countryside, seeking better medical care for me or were they running out of funds? They never did tell me, but now I believe it was the last case.

---

11 Decades later three of my Japanese-into-English literary translations were published.

15

SENNIN BARI

Our family had just moved to Osaka in spring 1943, and everywhere we went we heard women calling out: *"Sennin bari! Sennin bari!* Won't you please make a knot on my *sennin bari* for my son, husband, brother?" It was an ubiquitous plea by women on behalf of their loved ones leaving for the front. The women stationed themselves at streetcar stops, subway entrances, outside shops and on street corners, any place where many people passed by or congregated. *Sennin bari* literally means "stitches by a thousand people," and it referred to a rectangular piece of sturdy white cotton dotted with a thousand French knots sewn by women, and long enough to encircle a man's abdomen. It was considered an amulet that protected its wearer.

According to custom, each contributor could sew only one knot, except that one born under the zodiac sign of the tiger was supposed to make as many knots as her own age. No one refused to participate because that would be unpatriotic, but when I was tired I deliberately withheld the information that I was born in the year of the tiger, and sewed only one knot. I think the thousand red knots symbolized the flag of Japan—a thousand rising suns. (Decades later an American friend's aunt proudly showed me a trophy her husband had brought back from the Pacific theater. To my utter disgust and dismay, what I saw was a bloodstained *sennin bari,* an abdomen wrap that the man had taken off a Japanese corpse.)

In Osaka my parents both went to work for Father's cousin, Mrs. Miki, who owned and operated the Asahi Sewing Machine Company, which during the war was converted to a defense plant. Father took charge of the warehouse and mother helped cook meals for the workers. The same relative also provided us with housing. Many factory owners, Father's cousin included, added *yurei jinko,* (ghost population) to inflate the number of personnel reported to actually work for them. This qualified them for additional rations. Because of this practice and the largesse of Mrs. Miki's mother, my mother was able to bring home extra food, and we were never hungry as many others were.

As I still had symptoms of tuberculosis, Mother again took me to consult a doctor in Osaka. There wasn't much he could do for me other than to prescribe more rest and recuperation at home. As soon as I felt somewhat stronger, I enrolled in an English-language typing class and also began sewing lessons. I also studied Japanese on my own and purchased English books at used bookstores to help me retain the language. It was just as well I was not attending school because as Japan started to lose the war, the government forced most students in cities to work long hours in armament factories and rural pupils to toil in the fields. When my health further improved in the summer of 1943, I too started work at the Asahi Machine Company. By then the Pacific War was raging and, in addition to compulsory labor for students, single women who usually remained at home were ordered to work in defense factories to replace men conscripted into the military. Mother feared that I might be forced to do some arduous task in a factory before I was fully recovered from my illness, so she persuaded Mrs. Miki to hire me as an office clerk. Typically, Mother was convinced that long hours of labor would exacerbate my symptoms and trigger a serious, if not fatal, relapse. Kindly, pragmatic woman that she was,

Mrs. Miki agreed and undertook to see that I was not overtaxed. Thanks to my mother's insistence and Mrs. Miki's sympathetic vigilance, I was able to recuperate completely.

My sister Shizue May unexpectedly came to live with us in the fall of 1943. I'm not sure why, for she had always been aloof toward our parents and me. Perhaps she missed Misae Rose, who had married and moved to Tokyo. The two sisters had been together all their lives, and Shizue May had always lived in the shadow of her more gregarious older sister, who was considered the family beauty. Shizue May was also pretty, but less strikingly so. Now she seemed friendlier and her new attitude pleased me. Unfortunately, the government soon caught up with her (everyone was required to register wherever they went in Japan to receive food coupons) and then she was forced to work at one of the Matsushita armament factories. Some days she came home totally exhausted from working the all-night shift. After a couple of months she somehow managed to gain a transfer to a factory near our grandparents' home. Her brief stay with us was to be the only time she and I ever lived together.

Jean, Seated, With Asahi Machine Co-workers 1943[12]

12 The Japanese superstition at the time was that if three persons were photographed together, the middle one would die. To ward off this possibility, one holds a doll.

After Shizue May left, John decided to leave Aunt Hamaguchi's home and transfer to a school in Osaka. When I saw him I understood why: he was so thin he looked half-starved. Apparently he either didn't get his share of food or whatever was apportioned to him was barely enough for him to survive, much less to study and do the rigorous calisthenics and military-type training expected of him. Mother hastily rounded up every bit of food she could find and he gobbled up everything placed before him. He soon gained weight and strength. Even with this kind treatment, though, he remained hostile toward our parents and me. In a fit of frustration he once struck Mother, and he often called me names—"Shit," "Beanpole," and "Yankee girl," among others. His anger seemed volcanic, ready to erupt at any moment. Naturally I resented the name-calling, but I realized he had suffered terrible deprivation at our aunt's home. Now and then, by way of peace offering, I brought what little treats we had—fried sweet potato slices, sautéed soybeans—to his room, where he studied. He never thanked me, but I had learned not to expect any gratitude.

As the months went by, younger and younger recruits and volunteers went to the front. At the Osaka train station I observed frenzied singing and dancing as young men gathered to see their friends off. This determined gaiety was probably fanned by jingoistic teachers at school and by patriotic songs like the following, one of those heard most often.

> If sent to the sea and a watery grave
> Or o'er land to an end on a grassy knoll
> Not a single regret will I ever have
> Should I die for the sake of my Emperor.[13]

John was one of the reluctant "volunteers" pushed into signing up by peer pressure. He was only 16 when he left for the air force.

---

13 An ancient poem from the *Manyoshu* (Collection of Ten Thousand Leaves), the first major anthology of Japanese poetry compiled some time around 760.

Our older brother Frank had already been drafted by the army and sent to China. Although all men were expected to shout "Banzai!" (Long live the emperor!) in the face of death, returnees from the battlegrounds admitted that the last cries from the dying men most often were: "Mother! Mother!"

No one in our household was prepared for our first air raid. Intellectually, we knew that sooner or later air attacks would begin, but to most of us the idea was just a remote awareness. On January 3, 1945, when the B-29s first struck Osaka, we ran to a small park across the street and lay on the ground face down, with our ears covered. *This can't really be happening,* I told myself, but I had no choice but to believe what I was hearing—the roar of planes above and the thud of bombs demolishing targets in the distance. We were to learn that once the planes were overhead we were safe. The most dangerous moments came immediately before they arrived above us, for then, depending on the plane's speed and the trajectory of the bomb, we were most likely to fall victim to a hit. In spite of all I heard, then and through subsequent raids, there was always a part of me—the magical thinking part—that "knew" I would survive and some day be at a much better place. I believe this sense of invulnerability helped me maintain my sanity throughout those turbulent times.

Immediately after the initial assault, most people in and around the city were jolted into preparing air raid shelters. Father made a crude one in the park across the street. First he dug a hole about four feet deep, after that he excavated smaller holes for support posts. Then he set down wooden planks for flooring, and some more planks over the shelter, covering the top with dirt. For the entrance he made a small door resembling a trap door with an exterior handle. Inside the shelter was enough room for only a few people to squat or crouch. The air inside was musty and damp.

When the siren went off, we listened for radio news of the approaching planes, and most people ran into their air raid shelters.

At the time, Japan apparently had some form of a primitive radar system enabling officials to give civilians information and warning about the estimated number of planes en route. The usual pattern was for a reconnaissance plane to appear, followed a day or two later by bombings that became increasingly intense as time went on. If a single plane was reported, I refused to leave my bed. Then Mother was beside herself with worry, running in and out of my bedroom, trying to persuade me to join her in the shelter. I said, "I'll take my chances if it's only one plane. I'd rather die in my comfortable bed than in that stinky hole." She left reluctantly, but she was too terrified to remain with me.

Neighborhood associations were formed to deal with the bombings. They issued circulars warning of possible fire hazards and cautioning us to keep our windows covered so no light would escape. They organized bucket-brigade practice meetings and whatever else they considered essential to minimize injuries during air raids. After a raid, elected air wardens checked their neighborhoods for injured persons. Women began to wear *mompei* (baggy pants tied at the ankles and waist) because full-length kimono hampered their ability to flee or to work efficiently in a bucket brigade. They also made padded hoods to protect heads from falling debris. In this time of crisis, people wore their long-sleeved silk kimono only for formal occasions such as weddings, funerals and other ceremonial gatherings. These, too, were scaled down, both as to cost and time allotted, since food supplies had diminished and the danger from air raids increased during daylight hours.

Slogans proliferated. One example was "The Walls Have Ears." This made most of us prudent in what we said. The official intention, on the contrary, was for citizens to report any suspicious persons and those who spoke out against the government. Another frequently disseminated slogan was "Bear More Children! Increase the Population!" Two of Father's cousins must have taken this slogan to heart for they produced 12 and 13 children respectively and for this earned commendations from the government. At the time I think the government's aim was to increase the population, not only to replace the war dead, but also to provide enough civilians to govern conquered countries in the future. We were also told to chew each mouthful of food at least twenty times, thereby creating a feeling of having eaten more than we actually had. I wondered how the government officials expected us to chew rice gruel, which was what most of us ate by then.

In between air raids, my friend Kazuko and I took private calligraphy lessons in the evenings. That was my one great pleasure during those harsh times. I practiced two or three hours a night and found great beauty in the art of rubbing the charcoal ink stone back and forth to reach the perfect consistency and darkness, then dipping my brush into the ink and stroking it onto rice paper. Ever mindful that each *kanji* character had to be perfectly balanced, I carefully applied pressure at certain points, then gradually released it to end with a fine tail. Attainment of a true symmetry in the writing of a poem in *Manyogana* (old-style writing) on a *shikishi* (special decorated paper for writing poetry) was an intricate and delicate task I set myself to master. Of the result my instructor said, "For a Nisei you write very well." Talk about a left-handed compliment! Eventually, because the air raids steadily increased in frequency, Kazuko and I were forced to stop attending the class—a sad day for both of us. One night incendiary bombs fell on the warehouse where my family had stored some of our valuables, and all my treasured poems went up in flames. I felt no regret or loss for anything other than my calligraphy writings, for I knew I could never duplicate those.

While I was working at Asahi, Miss Tanabe, a shy Nisei friend who had actually graduated from high school in California, wrote from Kyushu in the fall of 1944 to say she was coming to Osaka for a job interview at the English section of the Osaka newspaper *Mainichi Shimbun.* Would I accompany her? We went to the office together, and the interviewing editor, Mr. Hayashi, a warm, friendly man, talked to both of us. To my surprise I was offered the proofreader position sought by Miss Tanabe, even though she was more academically qualified. I felt conflicted about taking the job, but after some soul-searching I did accept. The work was more interesting than my clerical job, the hours shorter, and the monthly salary of sixty yen—equivalent to entry pay for a college graduate—was double my current earnings. My hours were an easy 11:00 a.m. to 6:00 p.m., including a dinner break, and the company provided our meals in addition to extra food rations. Considering the ongoing and worsening food shortage, the free meals and bonus food were a godsend to my family and me.

At work I joined three other proofreaders who huddled around a large rectangular table straining their eyes for typographical errors. I too grew bleary-eyed from the effort, but not for long: two months later the section chief promoted me to a translator slot. There I translated articles from the main Japanese press into English for the special edition which the company distributed daily to foreign nationals—Germans, Swiss, Portuguese, Jews and others. Most lived in adjacent Kobe and other nearby suburban towns. Here, for the first time since the war began, English-speaking people surrounded me. They were a motley group: older Japanese men who had studied abroad, native-born Eurasians, Nisei, and some other Japanese who majored in English in college. Ours was a cohesive, cooperative department and, as the youngest staff member at age eighteen, I found my colleagues solicitous and helpful. It was a time of incredible self-affirmation for me. Not only was I stretching myself by tackling a college graduate's job without a high school diploma, but I also knew I was performing competently as well.

What especially piqued my interest in that position was learning the truth behind the headlines—the reality that belied the propaganda. For example, we discovered that the official government figures for enemy casualties were routinely hugely inflated and those for Japanese losses greatly minimized. The phrase "Asia Co-Prosperity Sphere" was bandied about in articles written about "Japan's mission to save Asia from the Western imperialists." We wondered if the motives of our militaristic leaders were truly so noble.

Not everyone in Japan believed everything they read and heard. Right up until the end of the war, for instance, the newspapers parroted the government line that Japan was winning the war. The public, however, knew better—for had they not experienced the destruction of their cities, suffered staggering civilian losses in the bombings, and endured starvation-level food shortages? But most people were prudent and held their tongues, because the *Kempeitai*, (military thought control police) were everywhere. Few citizens were willing to risk arrest for speaking out.

By then, I think that many had lost their faith in the protective powers of the *Sennin Bari* to keep their loved ones safe on the front lines. They realized, too, that the *kamikaze* (divine winds) would not come to help reverse the tide of the war. And most disillusioning of all was their growing doubt in the divinity of their emperor!

16

TOKYO ROSE

"How would you like to be a radio announcer in Tokyo?" asked Mrs. Murakita, my co-worker. "They're looking for English-speaking girls to introduce songs, and you have a nice speaking voice. I think you'd qualify."

It was winter of 1944 and I had been working as translator at the English Mainichi Newspapers in Osaka for just a few months. A radio announcer! That sounded exciting! "I'd love to try out for the job, but I don't think my mother would let me go to Tokyo. Besides, where would I live?"

"They'll take care of you and find a place for you to stay. You won't have to worry about such details. If you want, I'll ask my sister in Tokyo to pave the way for you to go up there for an interview."

"Thanks, but I think I'd better discuss this with my mother first."

That evening when I broached the subject with Mother, she was adamant that I should not go, saying I was only eighteen and much too young to be on my own. It would also be unseemly for me to live away from the family. (In those days, girls normally lived at home until they were married.) Besides, Tokyo had been subjected to many more air raids than Osaka, and it would be safer for me to remain with her. Mother usually caved in if I pressured her enough, but in this instance, even though I did not admit it, I, too, was somewhat apprehensive about leaving home, so I did not badger her as I usually did to get my way.

When I informed Mrs. Murakita of Mother's refusal to let me go, she said, "I can understand how she feels. You seem mature for your age, but you are very young. If I were in her shoes, I wouldn't let my daughter go to Tokyo, either."

And those are the circumstances that saved me from the possibility of becoming Tokyo Rose. Only after the war was over did we learn that an infamous woman known as "Tokyo Rose" played records of popular American songs and made anti-American comments in between the numbers—all aimed at the men in the Allied Forces. Some of the target audience loved listening to "Tokyo Rose" broadcasts both for the music and for the great amusement they derived from the Japanese propaganda that they did not believe. The teasing and challenging way she delivered her undermining messages angered others. These men either turned off the radio when she came on or just listened to the music. The common people in Japan never heard the broadcasts and were unaware of the psychological warfare being conducted by their government.

Contrary to popular belief, Tokyo Rose was not just the single woman named Iva Toguri who was prosecuted and incarcerated as a traitor by the U.S. government some years after the war. Several other Nisei women who worked with Mrs. Toguri also read scripts prepared for them by American POWs who served as radio writers, but for some reason they were never tried.

Had I been accepted as a radio announcer, would I have been singled out like Mrs. Toguri, or would I have been let off like her co-workers? These are questions that come to mind as I reflect on the road not taken. I am so grateful that I did not go for that interview because I was much too young and naive at the time to fully appreciate the implications of that "exciting" job.

17

SWEET RAIN

The sirens wailed insistently. "Oh, not again," Mrs. Murakita sighed. She had been up half the preceding night in neighboring Kobe, her hometown, as it was bombed by B-29s. Now she must deal with another assault at her workplace in Osaka, in the English section of Mainichi Newspapers. A Nisei from Los Angeles, Mrs. Murakita had come to Japan in 1943 on a transfer ship with her husband, a Buddhist priest, at a moment when diplomats, businessmen, and certain professionals were being exchanged between Japan and the United States in the midst of the war. And now she was seven months pregnant with her first child, after twelve years of marriage. I helped her to waddle downstairs to the basement that served as our air raid shelter. Some employees from other departments had preceded us, and with more and more arriving, the place was soon packed.

It was spring, 1945, and recently the bombing raids had become more intense and deadly. Many targeted cities had already been largely reduced to rubble and ashes. The U.S. Air Force was displaying two types of weapons at this stage of its air war: explosive bombs, which took a heavy toll on Western-style buildings, and incendiaries, or cluster fire bombs, which broke into many pieces as they approached the ground and scattered over wide areas to ignite wooden structures, burning homes and shops to the ground.

From our basement shelter we could hear the burst of Japanese anti-aircraft fire mingled with the drone of planes overhead, and at times the ground vibrated sharply beneath us as an explosive hit nearby. Even though we couldn't hear the incendiaries, we knew they were falling as well because that was the established pattern for these attacks; and while our building was constructed of steel and concrete, we were still vulnerable to fire because we were virtually surrounded by wooden structures.

Mrs. Murakita meanwhile found a seat and settled into it gratefully. I edged down beside my roommate, Miss Hanada, a Hawaiian Nisei who had come to attend college in Japan and was stranded here when war broke out. At twenty-five, she was an extremely shy, timid woman who looked to me for comfort and support at the best of times. She smiled nervously, but neither of us spoke, for like just about everyone there, we too were exhausted from lack of sleep.

The general silence was broken a short while later when an air raid warden ran in, shouting breathlessly "Everything's...on...fire... all...around...us."

A wave of apprehension swept through the throng.

"This place will turn into an oven. We'll roast to death!"

"Shall we douse ourselves with water and make a run for it?"

"But we can't tell how far the flames will reach."

"We can't just sit here."

"Let's wait and see."

"We can't wait much longer."

The agitation spread and gained strength. Should we stay or should we run? Either way could prove fatal. Miss Hanada, pale and trembling, kept repeating, "What shall we do?" "What shall we do?"

Although I, too, was quivering inside, I put on a brave front and said, "Don't worry. We'll be all right." My voice sounded shaky to me, but probably she was too absorbed in her own panic to notice. The whole while, I was thinking to myself, I don't want to die yet. I'm only nineteen. I don't want to die!

It was an almost unbearably claustrophobic experience. Should I sit or should I bolt? Should I or shouldn't I? The thought of waiting passively for death to come was horrifying. No, I must take some sort of action. I made my way to an exit and there, just as I was about to pour water over myself and charge through the flames—a miracle! Outside, suddenly, it was raining. Not just a sprinkle, but a deluge. The heavens opened, and oh, how that rain came down! The ring of fire encircling us sputtered and steamed and died out. The crowd spontaneously released a monumental sigh of relief—that erupted into joyful "banzais!"

Later, someone told me that large firestorms create moisture in the air, bringing rain. I still believe that sounds like pseudo-scientific nonsense, but I do thank God, Buddha and all the other deities who sent us that glorious sweet, sweet rain.

18

ESCAPE

As we cowered in our air raid shelter in Osaka, a whistling explosive plunged straight into our house. Fortunately, this time the bomb proved to be a dud and a special bomb unit came to remove it. But the Allied air raids on Japan had increased steadily in number and intensity over the last months, and now Mother felt certain that the next one would kill us all. This was the last straw for her. Thus, in February 1945, my parents left Osaka to relocate to their country home in Yamaguchi Prefecture.

I could not accompany them, however, because I was in the compulsory-labor age group and could not leave my job. My co-worker Miss Hanada and I found a room to rent in a home in the small town of Minoo, about 30 minutes by tram from Osaka. On several occasions during commutes to and from the city, our rides would be interrupted by air raids that forced us to scramble out of the tram and seek whatever shelter we could find. Sometimes we ducked into a ditch or some other low-lying area near the tracks; there were no public air raid shelters along the route. Each time Miss Hanada turned to me and said, "What shall we do? What shall we do?" And each time I did my best to reassure her that we would be all right. Frankly I too feared for our survival.

Mother sent us dried fish from her seaside home, and thankfully, despite many disruptions and delays, the postal service managed somehow to deliver most of the packages. Since our officially allotted food rations were barely sufficient to sustain life, I started taking some of the dried fish to nearby farms to barter for rice, barley, fruits, vegetables or whatever the farmers could offer in exchange. So severe were the food shortages that many city dwellers were bringing to trade their luxurious silk kimono, of a quality no country folk had been able to afford before the war. The farmers welcomed my dried fish because for them seafood was in short supply. They never realized I was still a teenager because I could drive such a hard bargain. Since I brought the food home and Miss Hanada liked to cook it, our arrangement turned out to be ideal. She would wake me up in the morning saying, "Miss Oda, breakfast is ready," and then I'd roll out of my *futon*. She usually prepared rice-and-barley gruel with dried fish and some greens. When the weather turned warmer, we also went out to the fields to dig up dandelions and wild chives to supplement our diet.

As the tide of war turned against Japan, the Allied forces reclaimed Hong Kong, Singapore, Burma, Indonesia, New Guinea, the Philippines, and the South Sea Islands—Saipan, Guam, and Iwo Jima. They finally reached Okinawa, just south of mainland Japan. Even then our landlady, whose son was an army captain, refused to believe that Japan was losing the war. She claimed she had heard that blossoms miraculously appeared on pine trees somewhere in the country, a supernatural portent that the "divine winds" (typhoons, or in Japanese *kamikaze*) would ensure Japan's victory. Had not Kublai Khan failed twice in the thirteenth century to invade Japan, only to be defeated by the "divine winds?" Japan would certainly remain an undefeated nation.

Despite my landlady's misplaced confidence, songs of loss and retreat now played on the radio and were sung in schools. One in particular, *The Song of Rabaul* remains in my memory. The first of its five verses went as follows:

> Farewell to you, Rabaul, until we return some day
> My tears flow endlessly at parting
> From these beloved, memory-filled islands.
> Through the fronds of the palm trees
> I catch glimpses of the stars of the Southern Cross[14]

Rumors began to circulate that the Allied forces would invade Japan some time in September, and the government expected its citizens to fight off the enemy with bamboo spears to the last man, woman and child. In addition we were assured that the "divine winds" would protect us and ultimately the victory would be ours. At that point, with disaster clearly looming, I concocted a story that my mother was on her deathbed and I must go to her side. Mr. Kitamura, my sympathetic department head, signed the necessary form for me to purchase a train ticket, and in June I arrived home safely, to my parents' great relief. I felt guilty leaving Miss Hanada behind, but I was ashamed to bring her home because I could not be sure how Father would receive a stranger. At the best of times he was neither generous nor compassionate by nature. She had told me that she had relatives on Kyushu Island but did not want to impose on them. I figured she would have to find a way to impose.

On Suo Oshima Island, sweet potatoes were plentiful, but we had little rice and only a bit more barley. My parents and I usually ate some sort of rice-and-barley gruel with sweet potatoes added, and we often had steamed sweet potatoes as snacks. Friends and relatives supplied us with various other vegetables in exchange for the fish Father caught. Since salt rations did not come through, we made our own. We scooped clear, unpolluted seawater onto large

---

14 Rabaul is a major port town on the island of New Britain in the Australian Territory of Papua New Guinea.

plates, then let the hot sun evaporate the moisture, leaving a residue of coarse sea salt.

Our home was directly in the path of U.S. planes heading for Hiroshima and Kure Naval Base, and we often saw B-29 bombers accompanied by P-51 fighters. Once when planes filled the sky until their engines made the ground under our feet vibrate, I tried to count them until Mother shrieked, "Come into the shelter, or you'll get yourself killed!" She pulled me into the shelter Father had dug on the side of a hill adjacent to the house. On their return trips, B-29s often discharged leftover bombs onto farmhouses and small vessels on the Inland Sea. The home of one of our relatives was hit that way, but although the house sustained heavy damage no one was injured. As the bombs aimed at ships fell into the sea and exploded, various kinds of fish would be stunned and float up to the surface. Father quickly gathered these "gifts from the sea," and we feasted on some, exchanged a few with friends and relatives for other food, then salted and dried the rest for later consumption.

We ran for cover whenever the P-51 fighters were on their way back to their bases, for then the pilots fired indiscriminately on fishermen, farmers in the fields and any other moving beings. From their perch aloft the pilots probably thought of their targets only as "the enemy" and not as people with families, human beings with hopes and dreams like their own. Father always fished near coves so that he could speedily escape and hide should he be spotted. One day as Mother and I ate lunch, we heard shots overhead and quickly dived into our sweet potato cellar. From there, listening intently, we could hear one or two planes zooming back and forth above us and firing shots. Mother was petrified, and I told her it was probably a U.S. fighter and a Japanese plane engaged in a combat duel. But that was wrong. By then there were no Zero fighters left to protect mainland Japan, and what I conjectured to be an air battle was in reality a lone P-51 repeatedly strafing our house. Later Mother informed me that she and Father found hundreds of bullet casings on the roof, in the area immediately around the house, and on the nearby beach.

On August 16, 1945 (Japan date) Emperor Hirohito announced over the radio that Japan had surrendered to the Allied forces because a terrible new bomb had destroyed Hiroshima on August 7 (Japan date). Another like it had decimated Nagasaki three days later. It was the first time most of the Emperor's subjects ever heard him speak, and for me at least it came as a shock. His voice was thin and reedy, with no timbre of authority, and he spoke in archaic barely understandable court language. Until then he had never addressed commoners, who were taught to make low, deferential bows when he made one of his rare public appearances and to make obeisance even to his photographs. No commoner dared look directly at him, for he was considered a living deity directly descended from the Sun Goddess. Now he was saying that Japan had no means to combat such a deadly weapon and therefore had no alternative but to surrender.

I was secretly elated to learn the war was over. When my parents and others spoke sadly or bitterly of "Imperial Japan's first defeat," I wondered whether they spoke from the heart or merely mouthed wartime propaganda. Did they too harbor a silent relief? I dared not question, for I had learned to hold my tongue during the reign of the Kempeitai (Military Thought Control Police). At the moment, I rejoiced over my own deliverance. I was free at last. Free to dream. Free to have a future. Free!

19

I WALKED A LITTLE

In mid-September, just a month after the surrender, I was leaving to return to my newspaper job in Osaka as translator at the English Division of the Mainichi Publishing Company.

"I really wish you wouldn't go today," Mother said as she cast a worried glance out the kitchen window. "Why don't you wait until the weather's a little more settled?"

I didn't reply.

"Besides," she went on, "it's dangerous for a young girl like you to be traveling alone right now." Her unspoken fear, I knew, had to do with the newspaper articles warning women to head for the hills, cut their hair to resemble boys, and do everything possible to evade the barbarians because there was no telling what they would do. But I believed none of those scare stories. The Americans I had known as a child in Seattle were not bad people.

As mother cajoled, I watched ominous clouds racing northeastward, and my undergarments clung to my skin in the heavy air. I secretly wondered whether a typhoon might be on the way but quickly dismissed the thought, for I wanted nothing to interfere with my plans.

Knowing she could not change my mind, Mother released her characteristic sigh, only this one much deeper than usual. She then packed a lunch for me and walked with me to the ferry. Our family home on the Inland Sea was a two-hour ride away from the main island, Honshu, where I would board a train for Osaka. Mother waved to me from the dock, and I stood on the ferry deck until she became no more than a little dot in the distance, a fluttering white handkerchief. I believe she thought she would never see me again.

When I boarded the train in Ohbatake on the Sanyo Line, it began to rain. Inside the train I set down my suitcase, a small overnight bag, and a rucksack crammed with food and took a seat beside a stocky, middle-aged man. By the time we began moving, a driving rain totally obscured the view from the windows. As the storm increased in fury, gusts of wind, sheets of rain, and even crashing waves battered the train. The car shook, rattled, and creaked. Watery tentacles curled around us, appearing as if they would engulf us and drag us out to sea. My heart pounded, my palms turned sweaty, and I felt as though I might suffocate.

A man seated behind me spoke to his companion: "It looks like a good one. This is a typhoon!"

Buffeted by the raging storm, the train chugged its sluggish way onward until, after what seemed an eternity, we ground to a halt.

"Hiroshima. Hiroshima." the conductor announced.

I peered out curiously, but the rain limited the view. What I could see was only rubble and twisted steel skeletons of buildings. Nothing moved in that blighted landscape—nothing but wind and water. Hiroshima appeared to be a dead city. It was only forty days since the powerful new bomb had been dropped, and I knew many had died in the "pika-don," the blinding flash of light followed by the big boom. From our island home about forty miles due south we had seen the horizon light up, felt the ground vibrate under us, and tried to guess what was happening. None of us knew then the full implications of that bomb. Many initial survivors—some were relatives—came home to their villages soon after the blast with burns over parts of their bodies, their hair falling out—pitifully, grotesquely disfigured. Most died soon thereafter but, surprisingly, a few would survive.

Our train had been stopped for about half an hour when the conductor's voice came over the loudspeaker again. He spoke formally: "We are sorry to inform you that the rails to and from Hiroshima have been washed away. We have no further information at this time." That was all.

Dismayed, I mulled over the alternatives. I doubted the lines would reopen soon because of the already chaotic conditions in the country. Yet how was I to manage my luggage for any distance? I was much closer to my parents' home than to Osaka, but I didn't want to turn back. Some of the men began leaving the car. All the women remained seated, some obviously anxious, others impassive.

After nervously munching my lunch of sweet potatoes and dried fish, I briefly left the car to drink from the station's water fountain. I returned to my seat and debated a while longer, then finally decided: "I won't go back, I'll go forward." This decision was to become my motto throughout my life. Shouldering my rucksack and picking up my suitcase and overnight bag, I set forth. I could see many of the men—some were fuzzy-cheeked army recruits—striking out eastward toward Osaka. I decided to join them, not knowing that we would walk for two days and cover over fifty miles.

The terrain was torturous. Wherever possible we followed the railroad tracks, twice crossed sagging trestles whose supports had given way to swollen streams. With each crossing my legs trembled and I shivered as I looked down at the turbulence below, knowing full well that one misstep would send me out to sea. It was agony inching my way across, forcing one foot to follow the other. Seeing my plight, two young men took turns carrying my suitcase.

Where the rails were gone we took detours, climbing slippery hills, slogging through fields ankle-deep in mud, skirting landslides, pounding our own path as we went. Now and then I slipped and fell. One of the men invariably helped me up. My shoes squished in the mud and water. They rubbed against my heels, forming large, painful blisters. At rest stops I emptied my shoes and was barely able to squeeze my feet back in.

When night fell I followed the men into an abandoned boxcar to rest. For a fleeting moment I wondered if I might be assaulted like the young woman I read about who had been raped and murdered at an Osaka subway station during an air raid. But fatigue overcame me, and as soon as I removed my jacket, laid my head on my rucksack, I fell asleep. Sometime during the night I felt someone crawling up to me, and I kicked out as hard as I could. The blow must have landed on some strategic spot, for he slunk away and did not return. Also, while I was asleep someone stole money from my jacket pocket, but fortunately left my train ticket.

The storm passed over during the night, and the morning dawned clear and warm. Cheered by the sunshine, we started off again. As the sun rose, it became hot and humid. To slake our thirst, we drank water from possibly typhoid-contaminated irrigation ditches and village wells. As the day wore on, my blisters bled so that each step was agony. I was sorely tempted to toss away part of my luggage, but thoughts of the consequences made me grit my teeth and go on.

Toward dusk we finally reached the town of Onomichi, where we boarded a train for Osaka. I sat down and sighed, not quite believing that I was now safe. Then I borrowed some money from a fellow passenger for tram fare to suburban Osaka. As soon as I reached my quarters in Minoo, I scrubbed off two days' accumulation of mud, sweat and blood, then soaked luxuriously in a steaming tub.

My feet were swollen and raw, and I think I had lost several pounds. Despite my exhaustion, though, I felt a strange elation. "I did it, I did it," I repeated to myself, "I really did it!" Savoring my triumph, I drowsed off and slept for twenty-four hours straight.

An entire month passed before the rail lines reopened, and I have often wondered what happened to those who remained on the train. I later learned that it was one of the worst typhoons to hit Japan in decades, and several of its victims had washed ashore onto a beach near my parents' home. Mother told me that a young woman with a baby strapped on her back was pulled from the water by local fishermen and the women of the hamlet fed and lent dry clothing to the mother and child. The woman had sobbed inconsolably when she told them, "I had to push my little girl away. I couldn't save both children; all three of us would have gone under. Sachiko cried out, 'Mama! Mama! Help me!' Then she slipped into the water and disappeared." Because of this harrowing tale Mother was so concerned about my safety that she sent Father on the first available train to search for me.

When he found me he asked, "How did you manage to reach Osaka?"

"It wasn't too bad," I said. "I just walked a little."

I was nineteen.

20

THE AFTERMATH

Osaka and its suburbs were teeming with American troops when I returned from my parents' home in the country in September 1945. GIs were everywhere—on the streets, on the trams, and in the confiscated office buildings used as military headquarters and billets. Unlike the fearful monsters they were portrayed to be in the Japanese press, most were friendly young men. They were curious about their former enemies and extremely kind and compassionate with the little urchins who followed them around chanting, "Cigaretto, chocoletto, chewing gum!" This phenomenon gave rise to an ubiquitous ditty among the GIs to the tune of "My Darling Clementine" that went as follows:

Cigaretto, chocoletto, chewing gumu sanju (30) yen
Oh, please give me cigaretto, chocoletto, chewing gumu.

Some soldiers did give them candy bars and gum, and much more. But others sold their cigarettes on the black market or bartered with the natives for things Japanese, including antiques. Some also used cigarettes and chocolate bars to entice poor, hungry girls for sexual favors. In those days cigarettes were considered a highly valued commodity.

One day a tall, blond, fuzzy-cheeked young man approached me, and he used his Japanese phrase book to try to pick me up. "Ojosan, chotto matte kudasai." ("One moment please, Miss,") he began, then thumbed through his book, fumbling as he tried to locate the right phrases to converse with me. He spoke with a strong Southern accent and was obviously flustered. I smiled to myself as he tried one phrase after another in butchered Japanese. After I had let him go on like this for a while, I looked up at him and said in the Southern accent I had heard on the radio and in the movies in America, "What y'all want, Peaches?" Needless to say, he was astounded, and I left him with his mouth gaping.

Osaka was even more devastated from air raids than before I had left; major portions of the city had been demolished. People were cold and hungry, and many were dressed in rags. Homes that had escaped damage were overflowing with friends and extended family members, while the unfortunate homeless built shacks out of corrugated metal and whatever scraps they could find in the rubble. The influx of returning soldiers and Japanese civilians who had fled from the invading Russians in Manchuria during the last days of the war exacerbated these conditions. The squalid lean-tos reminded me of "Hoover Town," the cluster of shanties on the outskirts of Seattle we used to drive past when I was a young child during the Great Depression.

Many children had lost both parents and now lived by their wits, roaming the streets with no adult guidance or protection. At night they slept in subways and during the day they begged, stole and scrounged in garbage cans for food. I can still vividly recall one pair: an eight- or nine-year-old boy holding his younger sibling's hand and leading her somewhere. My heart lurched with pity, but before I could decide what to do to help them, they vanished from my sight. I often wonder whether they managed to survive.

After assessing the desperate conditions in the country, the U.S. government began sending surplus foodstuffs—flour, dried milk, canned goods and various other non-perishables—to their former enemies. This rescue effort enabled the Japanese population to avert starvation and the concomitant diseases that afflict the undernourished.

As soon as the war ended, anyone who knew a modicum of English, male or female, could pretty much take his pick in the job market. Miss Hanada, my roommate and co-worker, and I decided to leave Mainichi Newspapers in October 1945, and we moved to the town of Takarazuka, an hour tram ride from Osaka.

It was a beautiful town, wholly unscathed by the war, with a central park and tree-lined streets. In the springtime cherry blossoms were everywhere and a huge lavender wisteria arbor graced the park. We almost felt as if we were living in a small town in pre-war Japan.

Miss Hanada and I found work as interpreters/translators at the Takarazuka Girls' Opera Company, an all-girl academy and theatre complex. There young women of high school age learned to sing popular songs and dance in both Western and traditional Japanese styles and then went on to perform on stage. Taller graduates took on male roles and dressed in masculine attire. Many sought acceptance into this prestigious high school. The entrance examination was extremely competitive: the students had to be intelligent, good-looking, and talented in either singing or dancing. To those who attended their performances—especially to the younger girls—the Takarazuka stars personified all the glamour and romance lacking in their own lives.

In later years whenever I mentioned to Japanese friends that I had been employed at Takarazuka, they invariably asked me to perform, presuming also that I had taken on male roles, for at five feet four inches I was taller than most of my contemporaries. I found those assumptions most amusing because, in truth, I was so self-conscious at age nineteen that I consented to announce English programs for the Americans in the audience, only if I could do so from behind stage curtains.

The U.S. 123rd Infantry Division occupied Takarazuka after the war and confiscated some of the Opera Company buildings for their troops. And wherever there were American soldiers, the Red Cross was right there with them, providing coffee, doughnuts, cookies and other treats. The Red Cross also took over one of the opera company buildings. Company officials decided to invite the Red Cross personnel to a Japanese dinner as a goodwill gesture. Miss Hanada and I were assigned to act as interpreters, and geisha were hired to provide entertainment and serve the guests. The wardrobe mistress at the opera company "dressed" each of us in unaccustomed splendor.

At the party the Red Cross director, Mr. Larry Green, a Kodak Company employee on leave, invited me to work for him. I jumped at the opportunity as soon as I learned that I would have access to an unlimited number of cookies and doughnuts, for food was still in extremely short supply. My salary would also be substantially increased. I was to be the Red Cross interpreter as well as supervisor of over twenty Japanese workers. Thus seduced by promises of goodies, I left the Takarazuka Girls' Opera Company after only about a month and a half.

Seated at far right, Mr. Ichizo Kobayashi, Takarazuka President. Jean and Miss Hanada, seated front, 2 Geisha standing, Takarazuka executives and Red Cross Personnel.

To my initial disbelief and utter disgust, Mr. Green turned out to be what the GIs called a "wolf." He was a sharp-featured, heavy-set man in his late thirties or early forties who, at six feet four, towered over all of us. When he insinuated that it was part of my duties to accompany him to parties, I felt more than a little intimidated. I disclosed my misgivings to the men at the canteen, who promptly told me, "He's full of crap," and advised me to ignore the hints. I was deeply grateful to have this support, for I was still quite naive and unsure of myself. Thankfully, the Red Cross soon replaced Mr. Green with Mr. Corcoran.

Peter Corcoran, a Harvard graduate and social worker from Boston, was the antithesis of Larry Green. A handsome, muscular ex-football player, Peter was loved and respected by all his subordinates for his gentleness, compassion and generosity. Behind his back he was affectionately called "Cha-san" (Baldy), for although he was still in his early 40s, he was hairless except for a monk-like fringe. Peter himself once laughingly alluded to having "left the monastery." Soon after his arrival in Japan, he met and fell in love with a beautiful Takarazuka singer called Mineko, and I served as cupid/interpreter.

Peter Corcoran 1946

135

Mineko Yorozuyo 1946

She was flattered and completely charmed by this courteous, warm-hearted man's attentions, but her parents refused to assent to a marriage on the grounds that they could not bear to part from their only child. Naturally, Peter was deeply disappointed, but as a man of sensitivity he could understand and empathize with her parents' position, and accepted their decision with stoic grace. Mineko later gained fame as a movie star and also as the owner of a popular cabaret in Osaka.

On the family front, many changes were taking place. In early February 1946 Mother wrote to inform me that my oldest sister, Misae Rose, had died at age 24. She had stopped by our parents' home in late August on her way from Tokyo to our grandmother's home on Kyushu Island. That was the last time I saw her. Clearly she had come to say goodbye, for her advanced tuberculosis symptoms were obvious; she coughed constantly and was so weak she could barely walk. During the last few months of the war she had suffered untold hardships. Cousin Kimie of Yanai had accompanied her, for she could not bear to see Misae Rose travel alone in her condition. The two women stayed overnight and Mother did her best to prepare a festive meal of seafood with the white rice she hoarded for special occasions. Poor Misae could not hold down any food. Although Mother was concerned about her oldest daughter, she seemed more so about my welfare and repeatedly admonished, "Don't get too close to her!" After my sister left, Mother boiled all the dishes and chopsticks she had used and brought out the quilts she had slept in to bake in the hot summer sun. Grandmother Nakamoto lovingly nursed her favorite grandchild Misae until her death.

Misae Rose (22) 1944

Shizue May (21) 1944

Later in 1946 my other sister, Shizue May, married a young man who had boarded with our grandparents. The couple then moved to his home on Suo Oshima Island where he taught school. Older brother Frank returned from China with a bad case of malaria. To help alleviate his bouts of chills and fever, I requested and received quinine from the U.S. Air Force dispensary to send home. Brother John also returned from some military base in mainland Japan. By the time he had enlisted, Japan was in retreat and no longer sending more troops overseas or building planes for pilots. As for the extended family, all four male first cousins of service age died during the war.

One day in the spring 1946 John arrived unannounced at my doorstep in Takarazukka, saying that he could not bear to live with our parents and asking for my help. His attitude toward me had changed dramatically. He now treated me with respect and deference, behaving toward me as if I were his surrogate mother.

John, (19) Jean (20) 1946

What choice did I have? For a few months I supported him by letting him live with me, paying for his food and giving him pocket money. He made no attempts to search for work and stayed home, helping our landlady turn her yard into a vegetable garden to supplement the meager food rations. He was forced to leave, however, when our landlady's relatives moved in. Their large, Western-style home had been confiscated by the U.S. army for housing for their officers' families. Through Father's help, John found employment with the U.S. occupation forces in Kokura City in Kyushu. Father was employed there as an interpreter. Not surprisingly, he had returned to his former wheeling-dealing ways and made a lot of money, while Mother remained at the country home with Frank.

When the 123rd Infantry Division left for home in January 1946, I sought a bookkeeping position with the Fifth Air Force Post Exchange at the U.S. air base at Itami, near Osaka. Although I had no previous experience, I informed the young officer in charge, "I'm not familiar with your accounting system, but if you'll teach me I'll learn quickly." And I did. Pure chutzpah landed me what proved to be a really wonderful job.

I needn't have been overly concerned about my bookkeeping skills, however, because the two young lieutenants in charge, pilots Kline and Hurst, were casual administrators. When the PX inventory figures did not match, they made the numbers agree.

Lt. Kline, Sgt. Holt, Jean in PX Office 1946

When supplies exceeded the figures indicated, they distributed the excess—clothes, silk materials and sundry other goods—to their friends and to menial workers. I received silk pajamas, brocade material and other "gifts" from my bosses. To my mother's great delight, I sent her some soap, chocolates and other small items.

Lt. Kline was particularly considerate of all his workers and would tolerate no mistreatment of them. All military personnel were required to clear the base by checking in at the dispensary and the PX before leaving for home. One GI called me a "gook," not realizing I spoke English and was an American citizen. Lt. Kline ordered the man to apologize—which he did most reluctantly—before he would allow him to clear the PX. Needless to say, Lt. Kline was respected and liked by all who worked for him.

His generosity even extended to the use of his private jeep. When the jeep was not in use, he allowed me to take it all around the air base to practice my driving. Tony, our assigned GI chauffer to and from work, had taught me to shift gears, and I carefully watched him apply the clutch. With that little knowledge and experience, I took off on Lt. Kline's jeep. No one—not the MPs or the provost marshal—stopped me; they merely looked the other way or pretended not to see me. And with the bravado of the young, I even drove up and down the steep, gravel roads of Mt. Rokko. On weekends the lieutenant often let me drive him and his friends to Nara and other points of interest in the area. I was in seventh heaven!

Jean in Driver's Seat With Friends 1947

Working at the PX had other wonderful benefits. One GI was assigned to make fresh ice cream daily for sale at the PX, and I lost no time in becoming his chief taster. Each morning Harry (for that was his name) would bring me a generous sample of the "flavor of the day" which I would greedily consume. I never did return any samples. In addition, both PX officers and the sergeant who served as my office manager plied me with boxes of chocolates. All through the war years I had yearned for sweets, and now my longings were more than fulfilled. What a lucky creature I am, I told myself as I polished off box after box of chocolates. My blessings began to catch up with me, however, as I ballooned out of my clothes and was forced to order larger, and still larger sizes. My craving for sweets began to subside after a few months, though, and I gradually resumed normal eating habits and slimmed down to my former self. I still recall with fondness the sweetest job I ever had.

21

"PAN-PAN"

"Pan-pan! Pan-pan!" the school children shouted at our jeep. The name-calling was a daily occurrence as we passed on our way to work. The Fifth Air Force had assigned GI drivers to transport all their foreign nationals, Eurasian and Nisei employees to and from work. Though I knew the youngsters were merely echoing their parents' hostility toward women who fraternized with the former enemy, I felt insulted and angry.

"I wish they would stop that!" I said sharply.

Our driver, Tony, like the other passengers, was unfamiliar with Japanese slang. "What are you so angry about?" he asked, surprised at my outburst.

"I don't like being called a prostitute," I snapped.

In the early post-war years, conditions in Japan were still chaotic and food shortages continued to plague the nation. Many desperate women did sell their bodies simply to stay alive or to keep their families fed. They were different from the usual camp followers, these victims of the militarists' lost cause, and I felt sorry for them. But I certainly did not want to be classified as one of them.

In contrast to the general population, foreign nationals and Nisei were now privileged persons in the employment market. Special rations were provided for us by the United States and, in addition, we had our own mess hall and our own cook at Itami Air Base. I even brought food home in an aluminum lunchbox for the little boys at my lodgings.

English-speaking women in particular were much in demand. Foreign nationals or Eurasians or Nisei—we had our pick of men to go out with. Because I had missed out on the high school dating and parties which I had looked forward to before my parents took me to Japan, I wanted to make up for lost time by having fun. (I only learned much later that my contemporaries had been sent to internment camps). I enjoyed learning to jitterbug, listening to the latest popular songs, and flirting with the young men. It was a time of liberation for me—I was shedding the restraints of the stern and dreary war years. For example, on one occasion when a GI asked me, "How do you like Frank Sinatra?" I asked, "Who is he?" The man's obvious amazement gave me a clue as to how much must have changed in America since I left.

For all my enjoyment of life, however, I was sensitive to the animosity and condescension of the Japanese toward me whenever I went out in public with a GI. Their surreptitious glances and whispers irritated and troubled me. Sometimes their attitudes grew overtly hostile. One evening my girlfriend, Waka, and I and our G.I. escorts were on a tram riding home from the American movies when an off-duty policeman a few seats away called out to us, "Come here, you pan-pan, I'm taking you two to the police station."

Police station? Waka was shaken and hung back, and our escorts registered bewilderment. But to be challenged in public like this was more than I could endure. Impulsively, I pushed my way toward the accuser, flashed my American I.D. card and demanded to see his credentials. I then invited him to visit the Fifth Air Force Provost

Marshal the next day to clear up the matter. At that, our would-be persecutor trembled visibly, flushed a deep crimson, and mumbled several times, "Sorry, sorry for my mistake," all the while bobbing his head as if his life depended on it.

Later, when I explained the situation to our dates, clean-cut college students from the East Coast, they roared with laughter. I did not join them, for the humiliation of that encounter rankled deeply, but at the same time I was proud of having stood up for my friend and myself.

22

"I'LL NEVER COME BACK"

"Father Tibesar's in Tokyo," a friend informed me.

What can he be doing over here? I wondered.

Father Tibesar was the tall, red-haired Lithuanian priest who spoke Japanese fluently and who had been assigned to our Maryknoll School back in Seattle. During the war years he proved his dedication and commitment to former students through frequent visits to the Minidoka Relocation Camp in Idaho, where Japanese-Americans from Seattle were interned. He and other Maryknoll priests had worked tirelessly on the Nisei's behalf and had even arranged for some to attend colleges or obtain jobs in the Midwest and on the East Coast. My friend Anne told me how one of his colleagues had accompanied her to a Midwest nursing school to help her enroll. At the last minute, however, she had panicked at the prospect of being surrounded by "hostile white" students and wept until the priest brought her back to family and friends in the camp.

Now the war was over and I had just learned that he was in Japan to locate and give aid to former Maryknollers stranded here.

I contacted him and was pleased to find that he not only remembered me but also readily agreed to attest to our earlier acquaintance in Seattle. In addition, Mrs. Yamasaki, a family friend, wrote from Seattle, at my request, and sent Mother a copy of my birth certificate, thereby supplying additional proof of my U.S. citizenship. Meanwhile, I paid frequent visits to the American Consulate in Kobe, and after almost two years I finally received my passport.

Miss Hanada, my former roommate and colleague from Mainichi Newspapers, returned to her hometown near Hilo on Hawaii's Big Island in the spring of 1947 on one of the first ships launched by American President Lines after the war. I am not sure what she told her parents, but apparently she spoke very well of me, because they seemed to be so grateful that I was there to share the terrors and hardships of the war with their daughter that they sent me a first-class steamship ticket to Honolulu. I appreciated their generosity—although I knew it was a loan—but I promptly exchanged the ticket for a second-class passage so I could collect the difference as a refund to use when I reached America. Because the peace treaty between Japan and the Allied countries had not yet been signed (it would be signed in 1952), there was no official monetary exchange between the two countries and no one could take currency out of Japan.

In preparation for the voyage I also bought black-market dollars from GIs, and Lt. Kline, my PX boss, kindly offered to send this money to me in Honolulu. On one occasion the provost marshal happened by as I was making one of my illegal transactions. I held my breath, certain that I would face some dire consequences, but luckily, he either failed to register or chose to ignore what he saw: he simply turned away and left. I breathed a great sigh of relief.

With two friends who also planned to study in the States, I went to the Mikimoto Pearl Farm on Ise Peninsula in the summer of 1947 to purchase pearls to convert to cash when we needed money. After each of us bought two strings of pearls, the

Mikimoto sales people served us some tea and showed great interest in our plans. Then they urged each of us to choose a couple of loose pearls to keep as souvenirs of our visit. Even sales people were much friendlier and less mercenary back then. In 1949 I sold all my pearls to Shreve, Crump and Lowe in Boston at ridiculously low prices.

Even as I was focusing my energies on returning to America, others were busy plotting a future life for me in Japan. From the time I was seventeen I had been receiving marriage proposals through family friends, relatives, and other go-betweens. Several families now saw me as a likely candidate to bring prosperity to any household because of my bilingual skills and concomitant earning power in the postwar economy. I declined all offers because I certainly was not ready to give up my hard-won, newly found freedom, nor did I wish under any circumstances to enter into an arranged marriage.

And although I was making serious plans to leave Japan, a part of me felt guilty about abandoning Mother, who had counted on me for emotional support since I was a child. I knew I was at a crossroads and about to make one of the most important decisions of my life: should I yield to filial piety, settle for a financially secure marriage of my own choosing in Japan, and remain close to Mother, or should I opt for the freedom and uncertainty of life in America? I wrestled with my ambivalence and in the end, because I had seen so much mistreatment and abuse of married women in Japan, I decided to put my own needs first: "I'll never be a domestic slave like my mother and the other wives in Japan," I told myself, "I'll take my chances and somehow make my own way in America."

When I told Mother of my decision she trembled, looked away, and was silent for a long time. Then she turned to me and said only, "If that's what you really want." Each word seemed to catch in her throat. Her reluctance to let go of me was evident in her whole demeanor, yet to my tremendous relief she was not vocal about it.

Our relatives, on the other hand, were shocked that Mother did not try to stop me. They castigated her for "spoiling" me and turning me into a "headstrong vixen." "A young girl going off by herself to a foreign country will come to no good!" they warned. And through it all my mother still held her tongue. I too remained silent, but I thought, *I'll show them, and someday I'll make them eat their words.*

Mother and two friends—Mrs. Iki, my landlady, and Ryoichi Saito, my newspaper colleague—came to see me off when I left on the *S.S. Marine Adder,* a converted troopship, on September 21, 1947. There were no colorful streamers, no blaring music and very few well-wishers on the dock when the ship set sail. As I stood on the deck watching Mother, my friends and Kobe harbor recede into the misty distance, kaleidoscopic memories of my years in Japan tumbled around in my mind—the humiliations at school and the scorn of relatives who treated me like a mental incompetent because I initially could not speak Japanese well—my treatment as being less-than-worthy because I was a woman—the fearsome air raids and food shortages—and most of all, the lack of freedom to do and say what I wanted. All this I would leave behind, and I would be free. And I swore to myself, "I'll never set foot on Japanese soil again. I'll never come back. Ever!"

I was twenty-one.

IV.

RETURN TO AMERICA

23

HAWAII

My heart pounded as the small speck on the horizon gradually grew larger and larger until the contours of Diamond Head loomed directly ahead. Then the anxiety began. Would Mrs. Yoshino be waiting at the dock? My father had written his cousin to ask that she look after me when I arrived in Honolulu, but she had not responded. Did his letter go astray or was it simply that she did not want to be bothered? Or what if something had happened to her—some accident or illness? So many things could go wrong. *Oh, well,* I consoled myself, *there are worse places to be stranded. No matter what happens, this will be paradise compared to Hiroshima!*

As I made my way down the gangplank I heard a voice calling, "Miss Yasue Oda! Miss Yasue Oda!" And there at the pier stood the woman I knew to be Mrs. Yoshino. I breathed a great sigh of relief as she stepped forward and reached out to place a fragrant pikake lei around my neck. I thanked her warmly, then found the presence of mind to cover my pearl necklaces with the flowers so I could go through customs without paying duty. After all, I needed to hold onto as much money as I could for my living expenses and so, in more ways than one, this woman was a godsend.

The ship I was leaving, the *S.S. Marine Adder*, had begun its voyage in Shanghai where a large contingent of young Chinese boarded to study at U.S. colleges and graduate schools. In addition to the students there were White Russians and Jewish refugees who had escaped to China from Germany and Nazi-occupied European countries and were on their way to a new life in America. In contrast, we who boarded in Kobe were primarily Nisei returning home to either Hawaii or the U.S. mainland after being stranded in Japan for the duration of the war.

During the uneventful Pacific crossing from Kobe to Honolulu I shared a cabin with three other Nisei women though I had little chance to get to know them. I spent most of those ten days up on deck enjoying the company of the Chinese college students, especially one K.N. Chen, a tall, slender, good-looking civil engineer who informed me that he was on his way to the University of Minnesota to earn his Master's degree. At twenty-seven, he was older than most of the other students and six years older than I, and I found his "maturity" appealing. K.N. (who liked to be called "Ken") and I hit it off from our very first encounter and quickly became inseparable companions. We ate our meals together, attended dances, spent hours conversing while walking the decks or sunning ourselves in our deck chairs. To a young woman leaving Japan with almost seven years of bitter memories, this romantic shipboard interlude with an attentive, handsome new suitor was a balm to injured spirits.

Shortly before the ship docked in Hawaii, Ken asked me to meet him for dinner that evening at the Royal Hawaiian Hotel. As the scion of a wealthy Shanghai family, he indulged in nothing but the best. The next day he would sail on to Los Angeles;

and I would stop a while with relatives in Honolulu and only later go on to Boston. We would have this one more evening of fun before parting. I was, of course, determined to keep the engagement, but Mr. and Mrs. Yoshino were obviously taken aback when I asked for rides to and from the Royal Hawaiian Hotel for a dinner date with a young man—on my first evening as their houseguest! Although they tried to hide their consternation at my assertiveness and my fraternization with a Chinese man (the Hawaiian "melting pot" concept had not impressed the Yoshinos), there was no mistaking their disapproval. They withheld overt censure, I believe, because they had just met me and probably felt constrained to be polite. My guess is that they had expected a shy, conservative young person of passive demeanor and were totally unprepared for my independent ways. However, they made sure I arrived on time for my dinner date and even went out of their way to meet Ken when they picked me up later. Could they have been a mite curious?

"Handsome young man," Mrs. Yoshino observed when the evening was over. "And he looks very rich."

"Yes," I said noncommittally. I wasn't sure whether he had passed muster and I was not about to ask.

In the days that followed, I found Mr. and Mrs. Yoshino to be a kind, generous, hard-working couple somewhere in their fifties, who spent most of their spare time and money making up CARE packages for friends and relatives in Japan. Mr. Yoshino, a small, soft-spoken man, worked during the day as a gardener and at most other times let his wife take the lead in most things. She was a plump, pretty woman employed as a housekeeper by several families. Because of her outgoing nature and lively intelligence, she had mastered enough English to tell jokes as well as to carry on extended conversations—a most unusual accomplishment for a Japanese lady of her generation.

Kimiyo and Sohei Yoshino, 1947

The Yoshinos also were super-patriots; that is to say, their loyalties lay firmly with Japan. Mrs. Yoshino was particularly proud of the fact that she was a "daughter of the samurai," and she cautioned me that I must never forget that I, too, held this distinction and must never, never soil the name of *Oda*. She made a point of telling me how she made rice balls for Japanese POWs imprisoned on Oahu during the war years. Whenever she and her friends learned that prisoners would be in transit, the women quickly prepared rice balls and other Japanese comfort foods and positioned themselves so they could easily slip the food to the prisoners. "How pitiful they were—mere boys," she sighed. As she spoke, I recalled with sadness how I, too, had witnessed American POWS being force-marched through the streets of Osaka, the men so thinly clad in the cold that I shivered in sympathy and my heart ached for them. Many years later I learned that some Japanese women took pity on them as well and at great risk to themselves sneaked food to the men.

One phenomenon I discovered in Hawaii struck me as almost incredible. After the war, the Issei old-timers splintered into two groups: the *kachigumi,* who believed that Japan had won the war, and the *makegumi,* who accepted the fact that Japan had lost. Naturally, the two groups clashed whenever they met. One evening the Yoshinos took me to their *kachigumi* meeting, and even though I swore to the group that I had lived through the U.S. air raids and seen the devastation they caused, that I had witnessed the ending of the war in Japan, they flatly refused to believe me. These diehards would not, could not accommodate the notion that Imperial Japan had lost the war. I am told that similar schisms took place in Japanese communities in Brazil and elsewhere, causing much bitterness and rancor among those involved. For me, it was a surreal experience to see otherwise rational people deny what I knew to be reality. And I had wondered to myself why the Yoshinos continued to send CARE packages to Japan if they truly believed Japan had won the war. I chose not to challenge my benefactors on that issue.

Uncle John greeted me with enthusiasm when Kimiyo Yoshino took me over to meet him and his family, for I was the first relative from his side of the family to visit from Japan in almost 40 years. As my own father almost never spoke of his family I did not learn of Uncle John's existence until just before I left Japan. He searched my face for likeness to my father—which must have stretched his imagination a bit, for most people said I was the image of my mother. Now Uncle John was so overjoyed that one of his own had come that he insisted I stay at his home, took me on trips around the island, treated me to dinners and in general displayed an apparently uncharacteristic generosity. Mrs. Yoshino remarked that she had never known him to loosen his clutch on his wallet as he had for me. "He's sure happy you're here." she remarked. "I've never seen him like this."

His daughter Barbara told me that John was a domineering father and husband whose word was law within the family. Most likely he had picked up some of Rikiya's tyrannical ways inasmuch as he had no other role model in his early years, but he never showed me that side of his personality.

Uncle John O'Day and Jean 1947

Kimiyo Yoshino, a most garrulous woman, gave me more information about Uncle John's past. After Rikiya died, John was so heartbroken that he wept inconsolably and refused for a long time after the burial to leave the cemetery. Kimiyo took it upon herself to aid and comfort him in whatever way she could, but she was still quite young, working as a housekeeper and possessed of limited resources. Lacking financial support, John was forced to leave high school and take menial employment. His first job was as a deck hand on inter-island boats transporting various kinds of cargo. It was grueling work.

As soon as he found the opportunity, however, he applied for and got a job with the Hawaiian Telephone Company at its Kaimuki Station at Oahu. There, thanks to his industry and native intelligence, he worked himself up in a few short years to the top level of the company, becoming its chief troubleshooter. He could fix anything. John was a natural engineer and technician.

In 1925 he found himself in a solid financial position and ready to marry. He took as his bride Emily Iwamura, a Nisei elementary school teacher. A year later their daughter was born, and three years later, their son.

When the United States entered World War II, the government and businesses in Hawaii did not want persons of Japanese ethnicity working in sensitive positions, for security reasons. John, however, was deemed indispensable by the Hawaiian Telephone Company: they needed him to keep their lines working, so the head of the company asked him to anglicize his name and stay on. Thus John Masao Oda became John Mason O'Day and launched what I laughingly refer to as the Irish side of our family.

By the time of my visit Uncle John lived in a comfortable home on a hill overlooking Waikiki with his family: Emily, his schoolteacher wife, his daughter Barbara, 21, who worked at a bank, and son Donald, a high school student.

Barbara was thrilled at long last to meet a cousin her own age she could relate to; all her other cousins were young children. For my part, I was delighted to have a glamourous "sister"—a real-life magazine cover girl in fact—who knew her way around town and had a generous spirit. She set up double dates for us, and we found many opportunities to kick up our heels with a bunch of her congenial, self-confident, and fun-loving friends. They were very different from the mainland Nisei I had known, who tended to be constricted in their social behavior because of the pain and humiliation they had suffered at the hands of the Anglo majority. But here in Hawaii the ethnic Japanese, who comprised about 40 percent of the population in the late 1940s, were part of the mainstream.

Cousin Barbara and Jean, 1947

As Barbara drove me around Honolulu, I was impressed by how clean and unspoiled the city looked. It had a small-town ambience—no skyscrapers to block the view, the air fresh and unpolluted. "It looks safe," Barbara said, "But I've learned to lock my car doors so that strange men—especially military guys—don't jump in at stoplights." I never saw any signs of danger, however. The sandy beaches at Waikiki were sparsely populated, the Pacific waters clear and pristine, the skies a sparkling, vivid blue, and myriad flowers perfumed the breezes. We had fresh pineapple spears in our drinks, succulent mangoes and papayas for breakfast, and the thrill of picking ripe bananas directly off the trees. And I felt so-o-o exotic with a red hibiscus tucked behind my right ear.

Uncle John and Barbara suggested that I remain in Honolulu and attend the University of Hawaii. It was a tempting idea, to be secure with relatives rather than to struggle on my own in Boston, but the sterner part of me warned that I would probably grow lazy in the tropical climate and lose my motivation. *Besides,* I thought to myself, *the schools in Boston are of higher caliber and Peter Corcoran, my mentor, is waiting for me.*

Thus, after a fun-filled three–week vacation in Honolulu, I departed for Boston on October 28, 1947, on my first plane ride. Mr. and Mrs. Yoshino had lent me the fare which I promised to repay as soon as I finished college. In my purse I had $90 that Uncle John gave me as a farewell present, plus a few hundred dollars of my black- market money that Lt. Kline had transferred from Japan. With a mixture of excitement and trepidation I said goodbye to the Yoshinos.

24

AN UNCONVENTIONAL
ARRANGEMENT

When my plane landed at Logan Airport in Boston, three burly Irishmen greeted me on the tarmac: Peter Corcoran, Leo McGonagle, and Jim McGuire.

"Welcome to Boston," Peter called out. "Glad you made it." I was happy and relieved to see Peter, but a bit puzzled to see no women. I had no opportunity to pursue the question immediately, distracted as I was by picking up my luggage inside the airport while simultaneously parrying questions from the men.

We all drove to Marshfield, a small town on Massachusetts' South Shore about an hour's drive from Boston. There, in a large Dutch colonial house, Peter's housemate Martin Foley was waiting to welcome me in a friendly, albeit clearly inquisitive manner. It transpired that neither he nor the other men, apart from Peter, had ever seen a Japanese person before.

Peter led me upstairs to show me my room, a large bedroom with a fireplace and windows on the front, or south, and west sides of the house. The house itself was a lovely, four-bedroom structure dating from the nineteenth century. Sweeping lawns, acres of woodlands, and open fields and marshes, all part of Peter's holdings, surrounded the home. Typical of homes of the same vintage, the place had five fireplaces—two back-to-back in the dual parlors downstairs, and one each in three bedrooms. Peter had purchased the property shortly after his return from Japan.

Peter and Martin went into the kitchen to cook dinner while I talked with Leo and Jim, who plied me with questions about Japan, to which I politely responded. But, *Where are the women, Where are the women?* I kept asking myself. I could see no sign of another female presence nor was there any mention of one.

Because of the shock of finding myself the lone woman among four men, I began to fret. *What have I gotten myself into? How can I handle this?* In my naiveté, I had simply assumed that Peter had some female relative or live-in help in his home and I was stunned to learn otherwise.

Peter proved to be an excellent cook, and the four men and I sat down to a dinner of thick, juicy steaks; potatoes mashed with cream, butter and diced onions; and some well-boiled green vegetables. Peter had even purchased apple pie for dessert. I could see that he had gone all out to celebrate my arrival with what he considered a feast. Naturally, he had no way of knowing that I was used to fresh seafood, rice and lightly cooked vegetables, with fruit for dessert. To show my appreciation, however, I did my best to consume as much as possible of the fare provided, though I confess it was something of an ordeal.

After the guests left and Peter, Martin, and I went upstairs to our separate bedrooms, I was still a bit apprehensive as to what might happen. Thankfully, though, my fears proved groundless, for Peter lived up to the altruistic image he projected. He had grown up in South Boston, attended Harvard on a football scholarship, and was now employed as a caseworker for the Boston Welfare Department. Because he himself had endured a harsh childhood, he could identify with the poor and disadvantaged and therefore stood ever ready to extend a hand to anyone in need.

At times he would gaze out of his living room windows at his acres of fallow land and wistfully remark, "I wish I could sponsor some Japanese farmer and his family to work on this place. In their country they make use of every piece of arable land, even that tiny strip around the railroad tracks. Wouldn't it please them to have all this land to work and for free! I wouldn't charge them anything, but of course I'd accept some of their produce." He had been impressed, he said, by the diligence and honesty of the people he encountered in Japan. My guess is that his positive impressions of the country may have been fortified by bittersweet memories of his romance with Mineko, the Takarazuka singer.

Whatever his sentiments now, just before he left Japan he had said to me, "You're a bright little thing. If you come to Boston, I'll help you go to school." Well, I had taken him up on his invitation, and here I was.

Martin Foley, like Peter, was a bachelor in his late 40s from South Boston, a "Southie" as they said, and they had been friends since childhood. Martin worked at a post office in a nearby city. Although he also treated me with respect he was, unlike Peter, a bit of a tease and enjoyed baiting me as he might a younger sister. Since Peter did the cooking, Martin and I did the dishes every night and that is when he teased me mercilessly about the "love letters" from my shipboard friend Ken, who was now studying in Minnesota.

"And how's the boyfriend in Minnesota?" he'd ask almost daily in his version of a Scandinavian accent. "Missing you, no?"

And whenever I wore something new, he'd exclaim, "Now, would you look at little Miss Pinup!" Martin's remarks did not faze me at all, for to me both Peter and Martin were old men. After all, were they not a few years older than my own mother?

Because I had arrived at the end of October, it was already too late to apply to any college for the current academic year. What is more, I had no solid plans and knew nothing about college application procedures or the fees involved. No one in my family had ever gone beyond high school, and I simply felt I'd like to go to college, which seemed to me an easy enough thing to accomplish. Just as when I left Japan with a ship's fare that took me only as far as Honolulu I had merely shrugged my shoulders and told myself I would somehow find a way to get to Boston. Now in Boston I figured I would find a way to get into college.

Peter suggested early on that I drive into Boston with him and Jim McGuire, a co-worker and neighbor, and spend the day acclimating myself to East Coast America and exploring the city. I followed his advice, and soon fell into a routine of commuting daily with the men and walking the crooked, confusing cobblestone streets of Boston.

I learned to order grilled cheese or BLT sandwiches, hamburgers, hot dogs, or date nut bread with cream cheese for lunch. And sometimes when I tired of window-shopping, bargain-hunting at Filene's basement, or browsing through bookstores, I treated myself to a movie. Unfortunately, though, my solitary movie attendance was all too often interrupted by unwanted attentions from unsavory strangers in the darkness of a theatre. Sometimes a man would sit next to me and try to hold my hand. This approach was of the tamer variety. More aggressive predators furtively stretched out a hand to my knees and tried to explore beyond. Then I either quickly changed seats or, in the most extreme cases, left the theater.

On weekends Peter mowed his lawn, puttered in his yard or worked on his never-ending home projects. This he did with Martin's help, and also with the assistance of other friends who came to visit. His ambition, he told me, was to renovate the whole house.

An unexpected surprise was the discovery that he had a girlfriend, who paid regular weekend visits. Thelma Bragdon usually arrived about noontime on Saturday and left late Sunday afternoon. A bank teller, she lived with an older, unmarried sister in the home of her birth in Hingham. Both of her parents were deceased, so she no longer had to answer to them. She was still single at age twenty-nine, a circumstance considered disastrous by most women of that era. She was a good twenty years younger than Peter and quite aggressive in her pursuit of him, clearly intent on claiming him before spinsterhood claimed her. Unfortunately, although she had a pretty face her rather abrasive manner did not match her good looks, and her hubris alienated many, including most of Peter's friends. She made no secret of the fact that she was less than pleased when I appeared on the scene.

Despite her antipathy toward me, Thelma accompanied Peter and me on one of the first weekends after my arrival to see Plymouth Rock and other historic spots. After that, they returned to their regular weekend routine of Thelma baking some sort of pastry—often apple pie—for dessert, while the men worked on the house or garden. Peter usually stopped work a little early to prepare the meat or poultry, as Thelma readied the vegetables. To a casual observer I think they looked like a married couple.

After the dinner dishes were washed and put away, everyone gathered in the living room, where Thelma played the piano and Martin sang. In contrast to his rough exterior, he sounded like an angel when he sang. His was the first Irish tenor voice I had ever heard, and I felt transported by its beauty. On occasion Thelma harmonized with Martin in a soft soprano, and sometimes the rest of us joined in. I recall those evenings with fondness and pleasure.

At first I sometimes wondered what outsiders, particularly neighbors, might be thinking about our unconventional living arrangement. The answer was not long in coming. On one particular November Saturday morning, as I was busy dust-mopping one of the sitting rooms the doorbell rang. I went to the front door and found a priest standing there. Peter came from the kitchen and arrived at about the same time. I had never seen this priest before, and I knew Peter and Martin were not regular churchgoers. Why had he come? And without even calling? Were there rumors of something shady going on at this address? Were parishioners whispering about those older men keeping house with a young "foreign" girl? The priest looked first at me and then at Peter and asked sternly, "Is this young girl staying with you?"

"Yes, she is." Peter replied agreeably.

The priest lingered, making small talk, obviously trying to elicit more information about me. A verbal cat-and-mouse game began as the priest prodded while Peter amiably avoided elaborating on his household situation. After he left, Peter, Martin and I had a good laugh over the priest's visit to "save" his two parishioners and that "poor girl."

In the meantime my friend Ken, of the shipboard romance, regularly wrote me warm, loving letters from Minneapolis. He wanted to visit me in Marshfield over the Christmas holidays, he said, and would that be possible? I knew he expected an affirmative response from me, but his request threw me into a panic. How could I possibly explain my living arrangement to him? Peter was oblivious to my dilemma and simply told me to go ahead and invite Ken to visit. He could sleep in the spare bedroom. I wondered what Ken would think when he saw me living with two middle-aged bachelors, and Thelma visiting and sharing Peter's bed on weekends. How would it look to him? I felt so ashamed and embarrassed at the mere thought that I didn't know what to do. In the end I wrote to Ken with a fabricated story that I urgently needed to meet with someone outside of Boston during the holidays and could not possibly get together with him. He was disappointed, but he continued to write.

In 1949, however, he wrote to inform me he was returning to China. As the eldest son, he said, it was his duty to be with his family during times of crises. The Communists had just overthrown Chiang Kai-shek and China was in turmoil. We wished each other well, and never met again.

25

LONG ISLAND HOSPITAL

"It's high time I got a real job," I told Peter, my mentor, just after Christmas. I had found temporary work as a file clerk before the holidays and was pleased to receive a little income to add to the funds I brought from Japan. That money was almost gone and I knew I had to get serious about supporting myself and saving for college. Peter suggested I apply to become a nurse's aide at Long Island Hospital in Boston Harbor. He promised to help.

Thus on the first Monday of January in 1948, Peter accompanied me to Boston Harbor, where we took a ferry to Long Island, about a half-hour's ride. The island lies in Quincy Bay, in the middle of the harbor and is owned by the City of Boston. Its name derives from its configuration: it is 1.75 miles long and a quarter mile wide. It has a long and varied history. It has been used for farming; for raising sheep and pigs; as a military training ground; and as a fort, with historical buildings and cemeteries dating from the Civil War. In addition, since the mid-1880s when the City of Boston took charge of its destiny, it has housed institutional facilities of one kind or another: an almshouse to begin with, followed by a home for unwed mothers, then a hospital for patients with chronic diseases, as well as a nursing school and an institutional farm. When I arrived with Peter that day, the chronic disease hospital was the main institution operating there.

My guess is that Peter, who had many political connections in a town where "who you know" is all-important, pulled a few strings to get me employed without the usual waiting period. He introduced me to the medical director in charge, Dr. James Sacchetti, who greeted me with lively interest. He was a short, stocky man with a genial but gentle manner who was obviously surprised to see a young Japanese woman applying to work at his hospital. At the time there were very few Japanese living in Boston. After a brief interview, he referred me to the head of nursing, Miss Murphy, a stern-faced woman of indeterminate age. She looked a bit taken aback, but quickly hid her reaction and launched into a description of the duties of a nurses' aide. A nurses' aide, I learned, made beds, distributed food trays, fed disabled patients, gave bed baths, emptied bedpans, and cleaned and changed the clothes and sheets of incontinent patients and those with running sores. I was to work an eight-hour shift from 7:30 a.m. to 3:30 p.m. with time off for lunch and two short coffee breaks, one in the morning and another in the afternoon. At times I would have to work a split shift from 7:30 to 11:30 a.m. and again from 3:30 to 7:30 p.m. For this work I would receive the sum of $25 a week, plus free room and board. I was thrilled to think that, given these conditions, I could save most of my earnings for college. Also, because aides wore uniforms, I would not have to invest much in clothes.

I moved into the women's dormitory the next day. There I met Irene Dineen, a recently widowed, motherly 50-year old who was my assigned roommate and would prove to be a wonderfully supportive friend. "Just watch what you say, dearie, and you'll be all right," she said. "And at work be sure to do your share, but don't let the older ones take advantage of you just because you're green." Irene was full of all sorts of practical advice on how to get along in this female community and how to deal effectively with work issues. I felt excited and confident that I would do well on the new job.

The next day reality set in—literally smacked me in the face— when I appeared on the wards. The mingled odors of adult incontinence, sick bodies, and institutional disinfectant were overwhelming. Having never baby-sat or changed a single diaper in my life, I was ill prepared to take care of "adult messes." *How will I ever live through this?* I asked myself as I struggled to suppress my gag reflex. I needed to call up on wartime experience to help me get through this ordeal, I decided. Back then I had bolstered my spirits during air raids by concentrating on the idea that this was a temporary trial, and some day it would be well in the past and I'd be at a much better place. Now I consoled myself by saying, "I must endure this only until I go back to school."

Most of the staff and other employees turned out to be pleasant and easy to work with, and many went out of their way to help me feel welcome, smiling whenever they saw me and trying to make conversation. Most had seen only caricatures of Japanese—wartime cartoons of sinister buck-toothed enemy "Japs"—and thus might have been surprised to see that I had perfectly normal teeth, did not wear horn-rimmed spectacles, and definitely was not menacing. Carl T., a former Boston Globe reporter whose alcohol problem had landed him on Long Island as a hospital worker, seemed really pleased with himself when he called me "my little lotus blossom." I didn't have the heart to tell him that "cherry blossom" would be more accurate for a Japanese maiden. But then most people didn't know the difference between the Chinese and the Japanese. After all—don't we all look alike?

In addition to my roommate, another older woman—a doctor with a heavy German accent whose name I have forgotten—took a keen interest in me. Whenever she saw me in passing, she asked, "How are you getting along, my dear? Is everything all right?" I assured her that all was well, regardless of how I really felt. She asked where I came from and wanted to know about my family. Over time, I gave her a sketch of my bi-cultural background and my wartime experiences. She told me almost nothing about herself.

One day she said, "You look like an intelligent girl. What are your plans for the future?"

"I'm saving money to go to college," I replied. She beamed and said, "You'll do well. I know you'll do well." I was pleased by her encouragement and apparent faith in me.

In retrospect I wonder whether she might not have been a Holocaust escapee who was reminded of some female relative when she met me. Why else would a German-speaking female physician be serving on such a remote island in preponderantly Irish Catholic Boston? She obviously sensed some strong connection to me. Perhaps she felt we were fellow war victims or former allies in a lost war. I still have the Kodachrome picture she took of me in my blue and white nurse's aide uniform, surrounded by wildflowers on a hill on Long Island.

There were very few young workers at the hospital, but fortunately two sisters about my age and practically "straight off the boat" from Ireland were hired the same day as I. Mary Ward, the older sister, soon struck up a romance and got engaged to John McDonnell, one of the staff cooks, and the younger sister, Nora, and I became fast friends. The Wards' aunt and uncle had sponsored them to come to the United States. Since Nora and I had no other friends in Boston and we got along so well, we spent our days off together. We took the ferry to Boston to explore the city, enjoy movies, test various restaurants and shop—mostly at Filene's basement—for clothes. We both especially liked to try on hats, but as our tastes were still rather undeveloped our selections were less than sophisticated. Little did we realize back then that we were forming a friendship that would last a lifetime.

Nora Ward and Jean on Ferry 1948

After several weeks I finally became more or less inured to the hospital smells. And as I became accustomed to the routines of hospital work, I was able to do my work proficiently. Although I functioned well on the surface, however, from time to time I suffered symptoms that I later learned were called "anxiety attacks." I experienced difficulty in swallowing, shortness of breath and heart palpitations. I wondered each time if I might be having a heart attack, but I kept my fears to myself for I did not want to appear incompetent in any way. Miss Murphy, the head nurse, told me she thought I would make a good nurse and should consider attending nursing school. I thanked her, but informed her I was not interested. What I didn't say was that I had always hated the sight of blood and the hospital smells still put me off so badly that nursing would be among my last career choices.

All was not drudgery, however, for in the summer when we were on split shifts and free from 11:30 a.m. until 3:30 p.m., we often went swimming. Even though the water was icy cold, we paddled about and flirted with French-Canadian seminary students and priests who vacationed on our island. "What a waste," we women said to each other as we eyed the handsomest of the young men.

As Long Island was a chronic disease hospital, many of the patients were deadweight stroke victims, some of them hefty to begin with, and the nurses' aides had to roll them over to bathe them, make their beds or change their soiled linen. I weighed only about 110 pounds, and many of the patients were double my size or more. On one occasion as two of us were pushing and tugging at one of the heavyweights, an excruciating pain shot down my back and legs and suddenly I couldn't straighten up or move! What was happening to me? My co-worker called out to the ward nurse, "Miss Kelly, please help! Something's happened to Jean!"

Miss Kelly rushed in and before I knew it I was being transported to the employees' sick ward. Dr. Sacchetti, the medical director, came to check on me every day and made sure I was well cared for. He told me I had suffered a herniated disk. Nora and Mary Ward and other co-workers came to visit and comfort me. But I felt desperate. Would I ever walk again? And if not, what was I going to do? I was alone in the country, and what if I ended up permanently disabled like the patients in this hospital? *I want to go home! I want to go home!* I shouted in my head, forgetting how only a short time before I had sworn I would never, ever return to Japan.

It took me three full weeks to get back on my feet. Because of my fear of being stranded on Long Island as a permanent patient myself, though, my brave resolve to attend college began to crumble. I decided to take the more expedient course of attending a secretarial school, then returning to Japan to work for the U.S. occupation forces stationed there. They could always use another bilingual secretary, and I could probably get a free trip home.

26

A DETOUR ROUTE TO COLLEGE

"Mother's Helper Wanted" I read in the Help Wanted section of the newspaper. Under that heading was a job description: baby-sit a 3-year-old child, and light household duties. Student preferred. Compensation: room and board with negotiable weekly allowance. It was late August 1948, and I had just left my position as nurse's aide at Long Island Hospital and enrolled at Copley Secretarial School for a course scheduled to begin after Labor Day. Because I could not afford to pay for my own room and board, this job looked to be a likely solution to my needs. I could attend school, pay for tuition from my savings, and have my food and shelter needs met for just a little work. It seemed ideal.

I met the Shapiros for the job interview in their suburban home, a duplex in Newton, approximately 20 minutes by bus from Copley Square in Boston. They were both immediately interested in my background.

Mr. Shapiro asked, "What are you doing so far from home?"

"When I left home I had planned to go to college," I explained, "but now I'm so homesick I've enrolled in a secretarial school in Boston so I can go home by getting a job with the U.S. occupation forces in Japan. I'll be here for the school year."

The couple asked a few more questions, conferred briefly with each other in another room, then returned to say they wanted to hire me. They offered me room and board, plus bus fare and $5.00 weekly allowance. After school I was to baby-sit their daughter Sally, bathe her at night, do the dinner dishes and help out with whatever else needed to be done. I would not have to clean house, for they had a cleaning woman who came weekly. I moved into their home a few days later.

Alice and Mark Shapiro were both still in their early 20s. Apparently they had felt they could not wait to complete college before getting married, so both dropped out of school, she from New York University and he from Harvard. Her affluent parents had not only purchased their duplex for them and but also set up Mark in a haberdashery business in downtown Boston. Thus, for such a young couple, they enjoyed a most comfortable lifestyle. Alice was expecting her second child, and judging from the protrusion of her abdomen, she hadn't long to wait.

They lived in the upstairs unit and his brother, a resident at one of the Boston hospitals, paid them rent for the first-floor flat. The brother's wife, a Radcliffe graduate, was a serious-faced woman who appeared to disapprove of Alice, and the two families seldom interacted beyond perfunctory exchanges. My room was a walled-in porch barely large enough to contain a single bed and a dresser. Because it lacked central heating, the Shapiros supplied an electric space heater for me to use during the winter months.

After Labor Day I began my commute to Copley Secretarial School, located on the second floor of an old building directly across from the Copley Plaza Hotel and kitty-corner from the Boston Main Library. The school was established and run by a Boston-born and -bred Nisei, Miss Oyama. She was a plump, middle-aged woman. Her staff was composed of just two others: a secretary and an accounting teacher. She herself taught shorthand and typing to our class of ten to twelve students. And although Miss Oyama was pleasant enough in general, she was such a stickler for detail that we students held our breath whenever she came around to check our work. The accounting teacher, an easy-going, friendly man, made more palatable a subject that could have bored most of us to tears.

My classmates were all high school graduates from working-class families, good solid citizens who were kind and helpful. I was interested to notice that there were two male students among us, a handsome Italian named Tony, with a beguiling smile and charming personality, and a blond fellow called Bill, more reserved but also pleasant. I wondered why the two men chose to go into what was considered a woman's field. I made friends with most of the students, socialized with them during lunch hours, was invited to dinner by a few and, overall, enjoyed associating with my new friends.

With Some Classmates From Copley Secretarial School 1949

Since I had already learned to use a typewriter in Osaka while I was recuperating from tuberculosis, typing classes presented no problem, although I never became a crack typist like some who were more dexterous. Shorthand also was a breeze, for I had memorized hundreds of complex *kanji* Japanese characters, and shorthand was simple by comparison. Nor were the accounting classes challenging, so I learned no more than I needed to in that class and did little homework. In my spare time at home I read and listened to the radio.

A social highlight for me during that time was meeting the Abos. Mr. and Mrs. Abo ran a small walk-down Oriental gift shop on the corner of Copley Square. Before the war they had owned a large store offering quality Japanese and Chinese antiques and jewelry, and had done well financially. According to Mrs. Abo, during their heyday they were invited to many social events where they dressed in evening clothes and hobnobbed with the Boston elite. During the war, however, when they could no longer import goods from the Orient, their business dwindled and they were forced to downsize and relocate to their present shop. Mr. Abo was a stern-faced man whose main interest seemed to be making money. He seldom smiled and never displayed a hint of humor. On the other hand, his wife was warm, outgoing and interested in all who came into her orbit. A tiny woman of four feet eight or nine with a deep dimple in each cheek, many described her as "cute as a button." What was unusual about her compared to others of her generation was that she spoke English well and read not only the daily newspapers but the daily racing forms as well. If I caught her studying a racing form, she'd try to hide it from me. "I'm just reading it," she would say. "You know, it's not good to gamble. Don't you ever bet on horses!" An Irish cabbie bookie frequently stopped by to pick up her bets. I found her surreptitious gambling quite amusing.

Because of her engaging personality, many Japanese war brides visited the shop just to talk with a sympathetic older woman from the home country. She was always kind to these young women trying to adapt to a totally alien culture, and from time to time she told me about their adjustment problems, some of which were sad, many rather funny. I vividly recall one such tale about a war bride who had married into an Italian family. She came in one day complaining to Mrs. Abo, "All they eat is *udon! udon! udon!* (Japanese noodles). They never eat rice, I'm dying to have some rice!" She knew nothing about spaghetti, for up to that time there were Italian restaurants only in major cities in Japan; this was before spaghetti and many of its pasta varieties became so well known as they are today.

Mrs. Abo had left her beloved only child from her first marriage with her own family in Japan, and missed her sorely. She hadn't seen this by-then adult daughter for many years, but her present husband would not allow her to visit Japan, and having been indoctrinated to obey her husband, she did not challenge his authority. However, when she learned that I was alone in the country, she took me under her wing and in a sense made me her surrogate daughter. On weekends she often invited me to her home, where she prepared delicious Japanese meals. There, the pet parrot, Polly, would join us, sitting on Mr. Abo's shoulders. A friend had given the parrot to the couple and they were not certain of her age. But she definitely was old. She was arthritic, so the staid Mr. Abo tenderly massaged her legs, and when the weather was hot he gave her a lukewarm shower to cool her off. Indeed, he was far more solicitous of the bird than he was of his own wife. Mrs. Abo also doted on Polly. She said that Polly did not like birdseed, so she sliced off the kernels from corncobs, and the indulged bird ate only the sweet center of each kernel. On most occasions when I visited her shop she had some sort of treat waiting for me. I think I provided a measure of consolation to her as the one person to whom she could confide her longing for her absent daughter.

On the home front, I was kept busy taking care of curly-haired, bright-eyed little Sally and, later, the newborn Amy. Initially, the Shapiros hired a nurse when they brought Amy home from the hospital, but after the nurse was released, I took both Sally and Amy for walks. While Amy slept, I played games with Sally, read to her and kept her out of her mother's way. When Alice was home she doted on her infant, crooning, "Once in love with Amy, always in love with Amy..." while brushing aside Sally when she clamored for her mother's attention. Sally then turned to me for comfort. After dinner I did the dishes and helped with small household chores. I was tremendously relieved to find that Mrs. Shapiro liked to cook, for otherwise it would have been disastrous, since I had never learned: Mother always chased me out of the kitchen with the promise, "You can learn to cook when you get married."

Alice's parents often came to visit from New York. I thought they were unusually indulgent of their only daughter. They treated her to a trip to New York to buy a whole new wardrobe shortly after Amy was born. In addition, they gave her a console television, a rare and costly possession at the time. Even I gained from her parents' generosity, for Alice passed down to me her pre-Amy clothes, some hardly worn.

On Jewish holidays Alice's mother made gefilte fish, chicken liver pate and chicken soup with matzo balls, among other specialties. She was an old-fashioned cook who created everything "from scratch," and as her mother had taught her, Alice also was an accomplished cook. I learned to love Jewish food. Until I lived with the Shapiros I had not even known the difference between Jews and gentiles, so on the whole living with the family was a fulfilling educational experience for me.

Alice's mother was what one might call a stereotypical Jewish grandmother in that she wanted to feed people, especially her grandchildren—her little treasures. Sally was a healthy, but thin, wiry child who Grandmother thought should be fattened up. She continually prodded Sally to eat more, often spoon-feeding her when the child was quite capable of feeding herself. On one occasion, Sally was seated on the toilet after dinner and her grandmother went so far as to follow her into the bathroom carrying Sally's unfinished dinner and keep spooning and coaxing, "Now, just one more bite for Grandma. One little bite. That's a good girl." I was appalled. *In one end and out the other,* I thought.

By early spring I had begun to feel at ease in my surroundings and my homesickness had almost evaporated. I found the classes at school boring and didn't relish the thought of making secretarial work my career. When I told Mr. Shapiro of my change of heart and my desire to attend college instead, he enthusiastically endorsed my new goal. "I have a friend who teaches at Boston Latin School, and I can get mock college entrance exams and other materials for you to study for your college entrance test," he said, "and you can continue to live with us." True to his word, he contacted his friend, who supplied the promised materials. Thanks to his help, plus many hours of study on my part, I applied to and was accepted at Boston University for the coming school year. Mr. Shapiro said he was extremely proud of me.

I was grateful to the Shapiros for the year in their home, but I sensed that Alice might not be as considerate of me as her husband. There had been a painful incident during the winter, when I came down with a bad case of flu. Alice, of course, told me to rest until I felt better, but as I lay in bed feverish and achy, she kept calling me from the kitchen to help her with minor chores she could easily have done herself. She would not allow me the time I needed to rest and recuperate, until at last I felt so weak and desperate that I called Peter Corcoran, explained my situation to him, and asked if I could come to his house to recover. "Certainly. You're always welcome in my home," he replied. Filled with gratitude for his understanding,

I would rest in Marshfield until I was well again. Alice was quite upset when I left to go to Peter's, saying she couldn't see why I couldn't recuperate where I was. Because of her lack of understanding and empathy when I was so ill, I decided I would never place myself in a vulnerable position with her again. I realized that she was not deliberately trying to harm me, but rather was so focused on her own aims and desires that she was blind to what she was doing to me.

As soon as the school session was over, I left the Shapiro home and returned to work for the summer at Long Island Hospital, where I figured I could save most of my earnings for college tuition. I felt a pang of regret as I left, for I had become fond of little Sally and baby Amy. But I knew I would be better off in another environment for the coming academic year. That was the interesting detour that brought me back on track to college.

27

BOSTON UNIVERSITY

I dashed up the stairs of the three-story brownstone building on Boylston Street, and my heart raced with anticipation. It was matriculation day for the 1949-1950 academic year at General College, one of the 19 colleges comprising Boston University. On the second floor I joined about 500 others, some in one line, others on their way to another line, and still others chatting in small groups.

This school offered a new, experimental two-year program created by the Boston University president and modeled after the General Education program at the University of Chicago. Students were divided into two groups: those who met college entrance requirements and those who did not, for one reason or another, but appeared to have college potential. The college gave the latter group the opportunity to prove their mettle here, and assigned them to what was called Junior College and allowed them to take the same courses as the regular students.

Although I had passed the entrance examination with high scores and was one of those accepted into General College, I was apprehensive about my high school records, as I had not completed high school in America or in Japan. I came up with the story that my school had burned down during an air raid in Osaka, and the admissions people clucked sympathetically. I felt somewhat ashamed about the deception, but to placate my conscience I assured myself I was hurting no one and the school could drop me if I didn't keep up with the work. I was determined to succeed, though.

We had a core curriculum that required everyone to take concurrent classes in each of four major disciplines: Humanities, Social Sciences, Natural Sciences and Political Economy. All were coordinated as to the time period covered, to give us an overview of simultaneous developments in all areas. We took objective tests on all four subjects every two weeks and essay exams at the end of each quarter. Test results were posted on a large bulletin board. Inasmuch as everyone had an assigned private number and the postings showed numbers only (no names), nobody knew anyone else's scores. Each time I checked my test results I felt certain that this time I must have failed. I could hardly bear to look, but each time I saw that not only had I passed but had done well.

Just before I entered General College, I came into renewed contact with my seventh grade teacher, Sister Mary Edith, through the staff at the Maryknoll mission in Boston's Chinatown. She had been my mentor back in the days at Maryknoll Elementary School in Seattle and was currently on sabbatical from her latest position (as a college professor) to conduct original research at one of the Harvard libraries. As soon as she learned I had asked about her whereabouts, she got in touch with me.

"It's so good to see you again," she greeted me. "I often wondered what happened to you after you left for Japan." When I said I was in Boston to go to college and had been accepted at Boston University, she countered with, "Why don't you go to Regis College?" She said she could arrange a full tuition, full maintenance scholarship for me and would also vouch for my academic ability at the school. There was a slot open for a foreign student, she explained, as the Japanese woman who had been attending contracted tuberculosis and dropped out.[15] When I asked what would be required of me in return for such a magnanimous offer, Sister Edith told me all I had to do was to start a Newman Club—a Catholic club—for Asian students in the area. I did not want to offend my kind friend, but since I held no strong religious convictions and did not relish the thought of attending an all women's college, I simply politely declined her generous offer.

Meanwhile, Lucy, a secretarial school classmate, told me that an aunt was looking for a college student to help her with childcare and some household chores. Was I interested? I checked it out and soon after that I moved to Newton Highlands to live with the Bermans. Helen and Charles Berman, were a couple in their early 30s with two children, Katherine, aged 6, and Martin, a two-year old. Helen had graduated from Hunter College and her husband from Yale, and they were much more intellectually oriented than the Shapiros. Although they also were affluent, they lived a simple lifestyle and were not conspicuous consumers. Mr. Berman owned and operated a cocktail lounge in Boston.

The usual contract at the time for a student/mother's helper called for 21 hours' work a week for room and board, plus bus fare. After classes I ironed huge piles of clothes, did the dinner dishes, bathed Katherine and completed a few other household chores. I could see that Helen had her hands full caring for Martin, who regularly banged his head against the crib headboard, and rocked back and forth. He still did not talk although otherwise he seemed intelligent enough. He did not interact with others like a normal child, however. Mrs. Berman bathed him and took care of him, and I had little contact with him other than baby-sitting for him and

---

15 I later learned that this student was Michiko Inukai, who would become a famous writer in Japan.

his sister on the rare occasions when the parents went out for an evening. Today I think Martin would be diagnosed as an autistic child.

Both Mr. and Mrs. Berman showed interest in my education and encouraged me in my studies. At times Helen even took time to read my papers and offer helpful suggestions. I particularly appreciated their treating me with consideration and for respecting my free time.

Theirs was a typical middle-class suburban two-story house built on a hillside in a cul-de-sac. The first floor had a large living room with a grand piano, a spacious dining room, a small kitchen with a breakfast nook, and a half bathroom. Upstairs were three bedrooms and two full baths. The bedroom assigned to me was not really a room at all: it was a walk-in closet with a small window—just off Katherine's room. Even though it was a little larger than the walled-in porch that I lived in at the Shapiro's, here, too, there was barely enough room for a single bed and a small dresser. I had to study and write my papers after dinner at the table in the breakfast nook.

At Mrs. Berman's request, I cleaned the house on Saturday mornings for three hours at $1.25 an hour, the going rate. Since it was a large house, I worked on one floor one week and the other the following week. In those days a thorough job was expected of a cleaning person. Helen taught me to get down on my hands and knees to scrub old wax from the bathroom floors with a steel scouring pad, wash the floor, then apply a new coat of wax. My knees and back were often sore and achy from the task. She also taught me how to vacuum and do other chores so efficiently that I became an expert at cleaning. She told everyone how pleased she was with my work, so I spent another three hours on Saturday afternoons cleaning house for one of her friends. For the six hours' work, I earned a grand total of $7.50. At the time a wool cardigan from

Jordan Marsh cost about three or four dollars. I did this extra work because I needed the money for books, clothes and school snacks.

At school I carried a full course load and worked an additional 15 to 20 hours a week correcting papers for Mr. Dale DuVall and Dr. Glen Wilcox of the remedial math and of the remedial reading offices, respectively. For this, the school paid me 75 cents an hour and during exam weeks, both men told me to take some time off to study but log in the full 15 hours as time worked. They said my work was worth much more than what I was being paid.

One morning I collapsed as I tried to get out of bed. I rested for a short while, then forced myself to go to class. On that occasion as well as other times of sheer exhaustion, I regretted having refused Sister Edith's help and the chance at Regis College. At one point I was even sorely tempted to drop out of school entirely. But my relatives' parting shot rang in my ears: "A young woman out on her own will come to no good." That dire prediction spurred me on. I gritted my teeth and vowed to myself, "I'll show them! I'll show them all that I can and will make something of myself!"

Dr. Wilcox noticed how stressed I had become under my heavy school and supplemental workload, and kindly took time to teach me how to speed read and skim textbooks and also how to perform well on essay exams. These tools and skills helped save me hours of study time through many a late-night struggle to keep up with the long lists of reading assignments and the many papers I had to write.

Professors from all the four areas of study took turns lecturing in the single large auditorium, after which we dispersed to classrooms in groups of twenty to twenty-five students for discussion sessions. One-third of our grades was based on our classroom participation, and reticent students were singled out to attend speech classes. I was among those so chosen, for I seldom ventured an overt opinion. To add insult to the injury, we received no credit for taking the speech class. The main reason I did not speak up in class was that I was listening to Mother in my head. She had told me repeatedly, "If you say nothing, no one will ever know whether you're stupid or brilliant. And don't ever say anything in public unless you have something intelligent to say." Thus, invariably, while I tried to come up with an erudite comment the topic under discussion had changed and I lost my opportunity. Also, the painful memory of being laughed at in class in Japan for a wrong answer or for speaking poor Japanese held me back lest I experience the same embarrassment again. And then because I had "skipped" high school due to illness and other circumstances and had gaps in my educational background, I felt myself at some disadvantage vis-à-vis my classmates. After taking the speech class, however, I forced myself to make at least one remark in each class, never mind its profundity.

As busy as I was, I managed to find a little time to socialize with my classmates during lunch breaks and between classes. It was a commuter school and everyone lived at home. I didn't feel conspicuous as an older student (I was twenty-three) because so many war veterans in their mid- to late 20s were there on the GI Bill. Some were married and even had children. It was a dating paradise for the women students, as the ratio of men to women was about six to one. I didn't have time for dating and partying with my crowded schedule, but I did enjoy getting acquainted with classmates of diverse ages and backgrounds: Irish, Yankee, Jewish, Greek and Afro-American—Dottie Greene, Nield Oldham, Evelyn Stein, Ethel Janis, Jean Sandridge. These students made me feel welcome and at ease despite my self-consciousness as the only Asian in the whole school.

Dottie Greene invited me on some holidays to her home in Franklin, an hour by train from Boston, and hers was to become my second Irish family. The Greenes were a warm, generous bunch; they even invited me to join them for a week's summer vacation in 1951 at a cottage they had rented on Cape Cod. While I was there another classmate, Nield Oldham, who lived on the Cape, called by to visit and took me to see the various scenic spots in the area.

Thanks to the Greenes, I enjoyed my one real vacation during the college years.

On Vacation on Cape Cod With the Greenes (Inset:Dottie) 1951

Although my grades reflected some deficit for lack of class participation, I made the Dean's List at the end of the first quarter; clearly my perseverance and hard work had paid off. When I had enrolled in the college I had enough money saved to pay for the first quarter's tuition with just a little left over, but not enough to cover the second quarter. I had gambled on the chance a good performance during the first quarter might draw some financial support after that. Now, trembling with apprehension, I approached the financial aid officer and asked for a tuition scholarship. I showed him my grades and the letter from the school notifying me that I had made First Dean's List. Then I explained my situation: "I came all the way from Japan alone in hopes of attending college in Boston and, since the peace treaty hasn't been signed yet, my family can't send me any money." I also told him how many hours I had worked at home and at school to put myself through college the first quarter. However, I held back the fact that even if he could, my father probably wouldn't help me financially because he did not believe in higher education for women.

The man looked at my report card and the letter, turned to me, and said, "You did very well. I'll see to it that you get your scholarship. Just keep up your grades, and we'll give you scholarships for the rest of your time at General College." My joy and relief brimmed over as I thanked him. He smiled and said, "Good luck, Jean. Keep up your good work."

At the end of the school year, I heard that perhaps as many as half of the class had been dropped by the college because they failed to meet the academic standards. I felt lucky indeed to have survived—and against fearful odds!

28

THE SOCIAL WHIRL

In September 1950, flush with earnings from three summer jobs, I giddily embarked on a shopping spree for new clothes. I would have more leisure time now with my tuition scholarship guaranteed, and I was ready for some fun. I wanted to make up for the past two years of working and studying with hardly any respite. And the new social life I envisioned would need a wardrobe to match.

As soon as the school year ended, I had returned to Long Island Hospital, but this time as an assistant technician for the pathology laboratory headed by my friend Claire. Hiring standards must have been quite lax, for the hospital gave me the job even though I had neither experience nor educational background in the field. Claire taught me how to do urine analyses for glucose levels in diabetic patients, and to read slides of urine samples for other diseases. I dubbed myself "chief wee-wee-ologist." I also helped with some blood analysis and did routine odd jobs around the lab. The work was physically much easier on me than my job as nurses' aide. Claire, of French-Canadian background, taught me to sing "Le vie en rose" in French, while Henry, a lively, funny fellow from an

Italian family, kept us laughing with his jokes. Harvard medical students assigned to the hospital for the summer dropped in to visit frequently, apparently drawn by the relaxed, friendly atmosphere in the lab. Claire and I flirted with them shamelessly.

Claire generously gave me time off to take on a second job within the hospital that entailed dispensing a new medication for a clinical trial being conducted on a select group of patients. I made rounds twice daily, chatted with my patients and made sure they swallowed their pills. I became friends with most of them.

On Saturdays I did secretarial work in Cambridge for a Mr. Nicholson, who ran a one-man office conducting a market survey for a well-known razor company. The job was not taxing and it paid well. Thus, by the end of summer I had a little cache of money to fall back on, which also meant I no longer needed to work for my room and board.

I learned through a friend that rooms were available at the South End Music Center for $4.00 a week rent—a real bargain! Although the center was located in a rather seedy part of town, the building itself was safe. At one time it had been the home of a wealthy family, and vestiges of its former glory were still visible in the neglected remnants of a formal garden on one side of the structure. Sally and Peggy Sprague, two elderly unmarried sisters who devoted their lives to helping the poor and needy, ran the administration offices on the first floor. The second floor consisted of six rental rooms and a single bathroom shared by all the renters. A huge community kitchen in the basement contained a gas stove, a large dining table, cookware, tableware and other culinary essentials—plus a practice piano. Each resident had a section of the refrigerator to keep perishables, and since we all had different schedules our cooking times did not often overlap.

On Saturday mornings Boston Symphony Orchestra members gave private music lessons in our rooms to the underprivileged children from the Greater Boston area. I learned later, however, that some of the students were actually from middle-class families and not part of the target population. That meant we roomers had to get up early, tidy our rooms and leave before 8:00 a.m. I thought that a small concession to make for our extremely low rent, though I often wished I could sleep in.

The renters were a diverse group of women. Patty Murphy, a veteran Army nurse on disability for a back injury, attended Boston University and was studying for her B.S. in nursing. She was divorced and had a small son being cared for by her mother in Providence, Rhode Island, so Patty went home every weekend to be with her son. She was a warm, kind-hearted woman.

Harriet Balcomb, a garrulous, eccentric assistant librarian, worked at the Boston Main Library. Her parents both taught at universities, her father at M.I.T. and her mother as professor of literature at one of the local colleges. Her older sister held a doctorate in physics, but Harriet refused to attend college although she was clearly intelligent and highly articulate.

Frances Schwab had been a pioneer social worker who held prestigious positions in her field, but she had somehow "burned out" and was currently engaged in low-level office work while she recuperated from her past stress.

Vi Cyr, a jazz pianist, was newly graduated from the Boston Conservatory of Music, where she had received classical training. She taught piano and occasionally gave concerts in small venues. Her sharp wit, breezy banter, and chic clothes made her stand out in any social gathering though she was not a great beauty. An only child, she called her parents in Maine on our hallway phone every weekend and rattled away in fluent French.

Edna Anderson, our Swedish resident, worked as an X-ray technician at Massachusetts General Hospital and also taught students how to read music. We all got along swimmingly except for one problem: Edna loved to take long baths in our one and only bathroom, and she often dozed off while soaking in the tub. We took turns banging on the door to rouse her, and eventually of course she would come to, but at times we were sure she had drowned.

Vi Cyr and I became the best of friends. She introduced me to a group of jazz musicians who held all-night jam sessions on weekends, drank a lot of beer, and generally made merry. As the only non-musician in the party, I thought of myself as their mascot. Joe, a bass player who was Vi's boyfriend, was very protective of me when some of "the boys," high on beer, made amorous overtures to me. I personally found Joe very appealing, but I never acknowledged the attraction because my friendship with Vi meant much more to me, and I would not cross that line. When "the boys" played at local lounges, Vi and I went to listen to them. We'd each nurse one drink all evening and wait for them to join us between sets. I was thrilled to be part of the swinging "in" group.

At school I continued working 15 to 20 hours a week for Dr. Wilcox in the remedial reading office and for Mr. DuVall in the math department, *and* kept my grades up. And since I now had more time to spend with my classmates, I attended a few parties with Nield Oldham, who always sat next to me in the auditorium for our lectures. He was a sweet, considerate young man and indeed my favorite friend at school. Unfortunately, however, he had little free time, for in addition to school that he attended on the GI Bill, he worked many hours to help support his family. But we did manage to take in a black jazz club once.

Shortly before winter vacation I received an astonishing letter containing—a proposal of marriage! It came from Bob Liu, a colleague from the days when I worked for the U.S. occupation forces in Japan, who was currently a U.C. Berkeley student. We had corresponded since we both arrived in the States if only to stay in touch while acclimating to our new surroundings. We had never dated; I simply considered him a valued friend. We hadn't seen each other for a few years and I responded with the suggestion that we meet again before making such a major decision. He promptly sent airfare for me to visit him in California.

It was with trepidation that I arrived in San Francisco where a joyful Bob greeted me. He took me first to meet his close friends in Berkeley, then via Southern Pacific train to Southern California to visit his American sponsors. I was welcomed warmly everywhere, and obviously everyone loved Bob. He truly was one of the kindest and most generous of men, and I guess I got caught up in his enthusiasm and that of his friends. Before I knew what was happening, I was engaged and wearing a large jade ring that Bob bought to seal our betrothal.

After my return to Boston, I mulled over my relationship with Bob. I really did love him—but rather as a sister loves a brother: there was no real chemistry there for me. Finally, I screwed up enough courage to tell him I had changed my mind and was returning his ring. Naturally he was immensely upset, and who could blame him? I had no wish to hurt him, but I simply could not go through with a marriage with someone who seemed like a brother—it would feel almost incestuous. Still, remembering the hurt I inflicted on him gives me pangs of regret to this day.

I then plunged into social activities with another group when I joined the Cosmopolitan Club, an international students organization in which the majority of members were men, inasmuch as few women studied overseas in those days. Thus, we few women who were members had our pick of dates. I had casual dates with people from all over the world; some pleasant, some fun, others frankly boring. At dances held at M.I.T. I learned from Brazilian students to samba and rumba. Those South American men were the best dancers I have ever come across. I had one date with a man from Vienna who kept telling me I had beautiful eyes, all the while trying avidly to seduce me. I said, "These beautiful eyes are tired, so it's time to take me home." And he did. I also went to a movie once with a Sikh, (turban and all) who had the strangest sense of humor: he laughed at all the wrong times. I never saw him again. A Nisei friend and I double-dated with two Chinese cousins from Indonesia who took us to the Barnum and Bailey Circus. My date, Sterling Chen, a serious student, and I became good friends. Years later I learned he had become a well-known journalist in his home country. I have forgotten the names of other members of the Cosmopolitan Club whom I met and dated—they have all become a blur of juxtaposed faces in my memory bank.

Another catalyst for social action was Nora, my Irish friend from Long Island Hospital. She and I had kept up our friendship after we both left the hospital. Now a nurse in Boston, she often invited me to join her and two of her friends, Esther and Elizabeth, when they went out on the town. Once they introduced me to a country/western bar where the music was loud, the crowd rowdy, and some customers wore boots and Western garb. This to me was another world, which I found both fascinating and repugnant, and although I did like some of the Hank Williams-type songs, the general atmosphere was a bit rough for me.

Another time Nora and her friends asked me to go to the North End for Italian food. There, while we were savoring our meal, four men from a nearby table sent over drinks and shortly thereafter came over to introduce themselves. Three of them were Marines and one an Associated Press photographer. They had just come back from Korea, and I surmised that their interest in me might be due to their contacts with Korean women while they were stationed overseas.

Bill, a very tall, powerfully built Marine, tried aggressively to coerce me into a date. His bulldozer approach frightened me, and I refused. Instead, I chose to go out with Frank, the soft-spoken, blond AP man with film- star good looks. I made the right choice, for Frank proved to be a kind, considerate man who always behaved as a gentleman. He called me "Princess" and made me feel special. We were to have many good times together; we double-dated with

Nora and her boyfriend, taking long drives to explore the country-side, and dining out and dancing.

Inter-racial dating was a rarity back then, and I could feel many eyes on Frank and me whenever we danced in public. One evening just as we returned to our table after a dance, a waitress came up to me and said, "The boys at the bar are laying bets on you—whether you're Chinese or Japanese. Which are you?"

Without batting an eyelash, I replied, "North Korean." It was at the height of the Korean War.

A few months later, Frank left Boston for another overseas assignment and I let my whirlwind social life wind down. My need for fun and excitement had been satiated for the time being. And as I was not emotionally invested in any one man, I thought now was a good time to give serious thought to my future.

29

ON TO BRANDEIS

"With your grades, you should be able to transfer to any college of your choice—Wellesley, Radcliffe, Smith," Dr. Wilcox said, "but you'd better hurry before they close applications. They may have done so already."

It was the spring of 1951, and for some time Dr. Wilcox, the Remedial Reading Department head for whom I worked, had been pressing me to initiate transfer procedures from the two-year General College at Boston University to some four-year liberal arts college. In the absorption and excitement of my social life I had procrastinated and neglected to confront that issue. Now I was down to the wire and had to take action. I was not interested in attending an all women's college such as Smith or Wellesley. They were located in the boondocks, far from Boston where most of my friends lived. But Radcliffe, I thought, might be worth checking out. It was a women's college, to be sure, but one connected with Harvard, and just across the Charles River in Cambridge, several subway stops from Copley Square.

"I'm sorry, but we've closed applications for transfer students. You're too late," the secretary at Radcliffe's admissions office informed me curtly. I started to berate myself. *Why did I put it off for so long? What shall I do now?* I knew that I would probably be accepted by the Liberal Arts College at Boston University because there, priority was given to intra-university transfers. That option didn't appeal to me, however, because the college was huge. I thought I would feel more at home at a smaller institution.

As was my wont during times of distress and uncertainty, I went to Marshfield to consult with Peter Corcoran. He urged me to apply to Brandeis, a recently founded Jewish-sponsored university, with notables like Albert Einstein and Eleanor Roosevelt on the board of trustees. In his days on the football team at Harvard, Peter had known Benny Friedman, the former Hall of Fame quarterback who was now head football coach at Brandeis. Friedman raved about the prospects of this school established just three years earlier, in 1948.

Peter was impressed by his friend's enthusiasm. "It has high caliber students and faculty members," he told me, "and I'm certain that in a matter of years it will become one of the top universities in the country. They're looking for as diverse a student body as possible, so I think you'd have a good chance of being accepted—and also of getting a scholarship."

I followed his advice and submitted my application. The secretary at the admissions office called me shortly thereafter and asked me to come in for an interview as soon as possible.

Brandeis University[16] is located in Waltham, nine miles west of Boston. I got there by taking the subway and transferring to a bus that dropped me off on the edge of town at the entrance to the 100-acre campus. From there I trudged to the top of a hill where I came at last to the Admissions Office. It turned out that the

---

16 Initially, it was to have been named Einstein University, but Einstein had a disagreement with one of the founders and refused to lend his name to the university.

Admission Officer was C. Ruggles Smith, the son of the founder of Middlesex University, the financially strapped medical school that had been sold to the Brandeis University founders. He questioned me about my background and seemed quite taken by the fact that I had traveled alone from Japan to Boston to put myself through college. At the end of the interview, he said, "We'll be in touch with you," but I felt certain from his facial expressions and his close attention to all I said that his mind was already made up. My hunch proved to be correct: in the ensuing days I received a flurry of telephone calls at my Boston residence from the Brandeis Admissions Office informing me of my acceptance to the university and of the generous scholarship granted me. The office was pressing me for confirmation that I would accept the offers.

In September 1951 I matriculated as a junior at Brandeis—and was not at all surprised to learn that once again I was the only Asian student in the whole university, just as I had been at General College. Here there were three black students, one male and two females; a handful of gentiles; two older male students; and two female Holocaust survivors. The rest were young Jewish male and female students straight out of American high schools. The junior and senior classes comprised approximately 100 students each, with quite a few more enrolled in the freshman and sophomore classes. To me this young population was quite a contrast from the predominantly male, older, war-veteran student body I was accustomed to at General College. On the campus were three chapels, representing three faiths: Jewish, Catholic and Protestant. Tongue in cheek, I asked, "Where's the Buddhist chapel?"

As there was a student housing shortage, a coed named Judy Dorf and I rented a twin-bed room from an elderly woman in the residential section of Waltham and for a few months commuted the short distance to school by bus. I was amused by the way "J.D." as friends called her, a bright, congenial young person from Philadelphia, handled her clothes. Each day as she removed her clothes, she draped them over the headrest of a rocking chair in our room. When the rocker was about to tip over from the weight, she scooped up the whole batch and took it to the dry cleaners. And when her funds ran low, she simply called her folks: "Mother, would you please put some money in the bank for me? I'm running low." *How uncomplicated her life is*, I thought to myself.

Even though I received a full tuition scholarship and had some savings from my summer jobs, I still had to pay for my room and board, plus clothes, books, personal incidentals and school supplies. Therefore I worked in the Admissions Office for about 15 to 20 hours a week processing application forms. Looking over the information on the forms was part of my job, and I was amazed to see that the average IQ of the applicants was about 140. I assumed that if the incoming students were that bright, those in my class, too, must have astronomically high IQs. I didn't know what my own IQ was because Dr. Wilcox had told me the test results wouldn't be valid for me because I hadn't attended high school in America and had no English studies while in Japan. *How can I compete with a bunch of geniuses?* I lamented. Once more I was as fearful as I had been when I had entered Boston University, certain that I would fail.

To further rock my confidence, I learned to my great consternation that in order to graduate from Brandeis I needed three years of a foreign language, and I had only two years left to do it. To meet that requirement I enrolled in a French class, but try as I might, I could not pronounce French; my tongue refused to cooperate. After a month I gave up and transferred to an intensive German class that met five times a week. There our instructor, a man from Vienna called Harry Zohn, divided his time between Harvard and Brandeis. All my classmates had two or three years of high school German behind them, and here I was starting four weeks after classes had begun, without knowledge of a single word in German. How could I ever catch up? Would I?

Fortunately, the required courses in my psychology major were neither time-consuming nor as rigorous as I had feared, and the semester system gave me more leisure time than the quarter system had. Also, since I no longer had to deal with bi-weekly exams as I had at Boston University, I was able to spend many hours studying German intensively, using three techniques—visual, auditory and kinesthetic: I looked at each word and pronounced it as I wrote it down, repeating the process over and over again until those words and phrases became a part of me. In class Herr Zohn spoke to us only in German. We sang folk songs at the beginning of each class, then in response to his command "*Uberzetsen!*" designating one student at a time, the student then translated the German text into English. Later, when the flowers and trees were in bloom, the class sat under apple blossoms for our German lessons. What a refreshing contrast to our dingy classroom! By the end of the second semester I felt at home in the German language—until I overheard one of my classmates remark snidely to his friend, "You have to wear a skirt to get an 'A' from Dr. Zohn." I was the only female in the class, and Dr. Zohn was a bachelor in his late 20s or early 30s.

The student housing shortage improved in a matter of months, and Judy and I left our temporary quarters in town to enjoy the convenience of living on campus. I moved into Usen Castle, the Brandeis landmark that served as a women's dormitory. The previous university owner had imported the castle stone by stone, from somewhere in Europe. I lived on the third floor in the round turret with my roommate, Alice Kraus, a drama major. My off-campus friends with whom I spent most weekends started calling me, "Princess." Alice's hero was Leonard Bernstein of the Music Department, and she tacked a profile photo of Lenny onto our closet door. Incredible as it seems now, we also had maid service; our beds were made and our room cleaned for us every day. Alice appeared to me to be very mature for her age, but even so I believe

I might have been a bad influence on this daughter of an ortho-dox rabbi, because I introduced her to pork and lobster dishes in Boston's Chinatown.

As for the food at Brandeis, the school cafeteria served out-standing meals, in contrast to the usual fare on college campuses. The cafeteria was housed on the first floor of the Castle. Wealthy Jewish merchants donated much of the food, and a professional chef supervised the whole operation. There were two lines, Kosher and non-Kosher, and students were allowed to have second help-ings and even thirds. Sometimes the friendly chef came around to our tables and asked if everything was all right. *Just like a restaurant,* I thought.

Around the same time as my move to the tower, the Admis-sions Office secretary told me that Dr. Abraham Maslow, the head of the Psychology Department, was looking for a student secretary to help him with his work. Would I be interested? I jumped at the chance, dropped my job at Admissions and soon was spending about 15 to 20 hours a week taking dictation and working on the manuscript of Dr. Maslow's first book, *Motivation and Personality.* He dictated in paragraphs, including all punctuation as he went along, and his writing was so well organized and fluid that it required little or no editing. Mr. Smith of Admissions remarked one day, "That Maslow has an IQ of 160." I could easily believe it.

Like so many students and other faculty members at the univer-sity, Dr. Maslow went out of his way to make me feel welcome. He also invited me to his home for dinners prepared by his cheerful, loving wife, Bertha. When I overheard their two teen-aged daugh-ters bickering over whose turn it was to do the dishes, I was amused to see that, despite their famous father's insight into human behav-ior, they behaved much like girls in any ordinary American home.

At the end of my first semester at Brandeis, still anxious about my ability to measure up to the standards, I was surprised to see my name on the First Dean's List. Admissions Officer Smith's eyes twinkled as he complimented me, "You made First Dean's List! Wonderful!" To my great elation, the same thing happened at the end of the second semester. I had somehow made it through my first year at Brandeis near the top of my class. Would wonders never cease!

30

ONLY IN AMERICA

Another move! I had just finished my last summer at Long Island Hospital, where I saved money for my senior year expenses. Also, I had requested and received additional financial aid from Brandeis. Now I could afford to share an apartment in Boston with friends rather than return to the dormitory. Eager to join me were Nora, my Irish nurse friend; Nora's colleague Esther; and Peggy, a Nisei friend who was a student at Boston University. They were all close to my age and pleased at the prospect of living together. The previous academic year I had spent some weekends with Nora and Esther at their place on Commonwealth Avenue and felt comfortable with our association. And Peggy and I shared not only similar cultural backgrounds but also a love of our ethnic food. I felt somewhat like a gypsy, though, for I had moved every year since I came to Boston five years before, in 1947. Life at the college dormitory was pleasant enough, and I had made a few friends, but almost all the residents there were several years younger than I and our life experiences had been so different that we had little in common. Thus, in September 1952 we four women moved into a one-bedroom furnished apartment near downtown Boston. We slept in shifts in the twin beds as Nora and Esther worked nights and slept during the day.

Our apartment was on the second floor above a lively bar and late at night jukebox sounds and bursts of laughter filtered up to us. We heard about the apartment from Vi, my jazz pianist friend, whose two gay friends lived in the apartment next door. Theirs was an attractively decorated place, very chi-chi. They quarreled a lot and one night, in a jealous rage, one man stabbed the other with a knife. The wound was not fatal, and the victim refused to press charges when the police came. Obviously, it was not the most savory of neighborhoods.

I commuted about half an hour to school, as did a dozen or so other students who could not afford the dormitory fees and lived with their families in Boston. Since I was now accustomed to the Brandeis environment and more confident of my ability to meet the standards, I was more relaxed about my studies. I continued to work 15 to 20 hours a week for Dr. Maslow, and he, like the professors at General College, encouraged me to take time off during exam week to study but to log in the full 15 hours as time worked. Dr. Maslow and I chatted in his office, and sometimes he asked me about my personal life. I respected and loved this kind, brilliant man whom I came to regard as a surrogate father. I told him of my personal conflicts as I had never confided with anyone before, and he referred me for therapy at Beth Israel Hospital Outpatient Department. There, where I paid a minimal fee because I was a student, a Dr. Payne helped me deal with some of my cultural conflicts, and with unresolved issues stemming from my traumatic experiences as a child in a dysfunctional alcoholic family. That was the beginning of my many years of psychotherapy that would eventually heal most of my childhood wounds.

All was not serious and grim, however; I also had some fun times. Two adventures with friends from Brandeis stand out in my memory. The first was a trip with Judy Dorf, my former roommate in Waltham, to visit her textile designer aunt in Manhattan. We took the red-eye special train that left Boston at midnight on a Friday and arrived in New York around 8:00 a.m. Saturday. Sleep was impossible on the unyielding upright seats, but what could one expect for a round-trip ticket that cost only $5.50, right? We wasted little time sleeping after we got to New York. After a brief nap at her aunt's apartment, we set forth to see a bit of the city but mostly to attend Broadway plays. Broadway! I could hardly believe it when I actually stood on that world-famous street for the first time. To take in as many plays as possible, we purchased the cheapest tickets available for matinee and evening performances, then rented opera glasses to get a decent look at the actors from our upper-balcony seats. We left New York at midnight on Sunday and arrived back in Boston at 8:00 a.m. to attend our classes, drowsy and bleary-eyed.

On the other occasion Annette Kaplan, whom I met while living at the Castle, invited me to her home in Brooklyn for the weekend. Her mother, a long-time widow, ran a toy store, and she and her niece, Annette's cousin, shared an apartment above the store. Mrs. Kaplan, who kept a kosher kitchen, welcomed me warmly. In addition to visiting the Metropolitan Museum and the Brooklyn Botanical Gardens, I had a blind date with a Nisei engineer pre-arranged by a mutual friend in Boston. When Kaz (that was my date's name) arrived to pick me up, Mrs. Kaplan gave him the third degree: "Where did you go to school?" "Who do you work for?" "What are your future plans?" and on and on. I'm sure she had my best interests in mind and wanted only to be sure his intentions were honorable, but I was so embarrassed I wanted to crawl into a hole and disappear. What's more, I felt heartily sorry for the belea-guered guy, who was probably meeting me as a favor to his friend. Kaz took me out to see some New York sights, escorted me back to the Kaplan home, then politely shook my hand and said goodbye. Small wonder he never called again.

Before long, life in our Boston apartment started to turn sour. Esther, who at first acquaintance appeared to be friendly and funny, did not wear well as a housemate. At times she behaved in such a boisterous manner that it was impossible for Peggy and me to study during the hours when we were all at home. She also liked to party at the apartment on her off hours, so that we had little peace and quiet. Added to that, the rental agreement, the utilities and telephone were all in my name, and I often ended up paying for long-distance calls I had not made. Thus, I reluctantly decided to move at the end of the semester, although it would be stressful to move yet again, especially in the middle of the academic year. This meant all the others must move as well. To top off my disgust with Esther, on the day we all moved out she took it into her head to trash the apartment, unscrewing all the light bulbs and smashing them on the floor, and wreaking whatever other damage she could. Nora had already left and was unaware of what happened; Peggy and I cleaned up the mess. I found it hard to believe that anyone could be so willfully destructive, and felt doubly justified in my decision to leave.

Evelyn Stein, a classmate from Boston University who had also transferred to Brandeis, came up with a lead for my next move. She introduced me to friends in Arlington who owned a duplex and had a room to let. I agreed to pay for my room and board. Paul and Laura Bennetti were a middle-aged couple, she a medical social worker at a Boston hospital and he a researcher at one of the M.I.T. laboratories. They had a six-year-old son, Billy. After moving in I learned they were avowed communists, and Laura was particularly proud of the fact that she had been the girlfriend of Harry Bridges back in the 1930s. In spite of her alleged communist ideals, however, she put on some decidedly bourgeois airs. She referred to me as her "maid" to her friends and expected me to clean her house on Saturdays and provide free baby-sitting for their son. I felt insulted and angry that she pushed such demands on me despite the fact that I was paying her for my room and board. Incredibly, she also took credit for my doing well in school—by what logic I do not know. Unfortunately, I had neither the time nor the energy to move again, so I resigned myself to enduring the situation for the few months remaining until graduation.

All this was at the height of the McCarthy hearings, when liberal colleges such as Harvard, M.I.T., and even Brandeis came under investigation as possible subversive havens. And because of the Bennettis' history of communist associations, Laura now became convinced that the FBI had them under surveillance from a house across the street. I'm not sure if that was true or simply her paranoia, but because of these circumstances and the possibility of becoming suspect through association with the Bennettis, my boyfriends were reluctant to visit me in Arlington.

In the meantime, I received a disturbing letter from my mother: "Your father is now living in Kokura City with his mistress and no longer sends money home. As you know, times are very hard here in Japan, and even though we own our home I have no means of support for my daily living expenses. I need your help, so please send me some money."

This was the first time I found out Father had a mistress. As a dutiful daughter, I had to respond to Mother's distress. I asked Dr. Maslow for help in securing another part-time job because I needed more money. I was too embarrassed to tell him the reason and he was sensitive enough not to pry, but shortly thereafter he introduced me to Dr. Edward Bibring, president of the Boston Psychoanalytic Institute, who was writing a book and needed some help. I arranged to work for him at his home in Cambridge, two evenings a week, three hours each time. The round trip from my home in Arlington to Cambridge took about an hour, so the new job added another eight hours to my work week. Dr. Bibring turned out to be a considerate, gentle man in the advanced stages of Parkinsonism. His quivery, tiny handwriting was difficult to decipher and his slurred speech hard to understand, but I did my best. He seemed pleased with my work and paid me $1.25 an hour. With my new earnings (which came up to about $30 a month), I was able to send Mother enough for her to survive. At the time the exchange rate was 360 yen to one dollar, the yen stretching much farther than the dollar. With some regret, however, I dropped out of the Honors Program with the knowledge that by not completing my senior thesis I lost the possibility of graduating with distinction in psychology.

In the spring, Dr. Maslow invited me to work toward a doctorate in psychology under his tutelage, and offered me a fellowship that would carry me through. I was deeply grateful for his generosity and his faith in my ability to do the work, but I was exhausted from years of juggling study, work, and social activities. Three or four more years of study seemed like an eternity to me then. I thanked him and told him that I would apply to a school of social work that would require only two years of graduate study. Smith College and Boston University both accepted me, and I chose Boston U. to be near my friends. Dr. Maslow was gracious enough to invite me to return for my doctorate should I ever change my mind. That I didn't accept his offer remains one minor regret in my life.

Shortly before graduation day, two conversations I happened to overhear stung me to the quick and dampened my spirits. One student I knew was telling her friend, "Jean's been elected to the Honor Society because she's Dr. Maslow's pet." I passed by and pretended not to hear. As Brandeis was too recently established to have a real academic history, it had yet to be accepted by the Phi Beta Kappa Society.[17] In its stead the university had created its own Honor Society, and I had been selected as one of five such honorees from my class. I felt deflated by that student's remark and wondered whether what she said was true. Was I being

17 In 1998 Brandeis University officials retroactively elected me to their branch of the Phi Beta Kappa Society. Unfortunately, I was too ill to attend the ceremony.

honored as a token, as the only Asian in the school? At home Mrs. Bennetti also disparaged my selection to the Honor Society, saying that she did not believe I really qualified. Since I thought deep down that I did not deserve the honor and felt so undermined by the remarks, I finally decided to skip the dinner given for the honorees.

Around the same time I heard another student whisper to her friend, "Did you know that Jean is 27?"

"You're kidding! She doesn't look *that* old!"

I felt like a veritable antique. Then I thought, *These pampered young things don't realize what I had to go through to get here. They just don't know!*

Stacey Sutermeister, the Admissions Office secretary, called me in one day to suggest that I write a thank-you note to a Jewish family who had sponsored me at Brandeis by paying for my scholarships. This was the first I heard about them. She said they would be attending my graduation.

"Can I meet them and thank them personally?" I asked.

"No, they wish to remain anonymous," Stacey informed me. I was not only astonished to learn about my benefactors but also greatly awed by their generosity and altruism. I still wish I might have met them.

On a clear, sunny June 14, 1953, Peter Corcoran, his wife and several other friends came to attend my graduation ceremony. There were 108 students in that second graduating class at Brandeis. Peter beamed as I stepped up to the podium to receive my diploma.

As soon as convocation was over, I joined my friends. Peter said simply, "You graduated with honors. I'm proud of you."

I smiled and said, "Thank *you* for all your help." I was immensely pleased to be able to show him his faith in me had been justified. Then I silently thanked all the others along the way who had eased my path. Five years and eight months had elapsed since I arrived in Boston. *Only in America would I have the opportunity to come this far*, I said to myself. *Only in America would strangers welcome me with such open arms and unstinting generosity. Only in America!*

Frances Schwab, Jean, Luba Geller (Holocaust Survivor)
June 1953

EPILOGUE

A few months after graduation from Brandeis, I married Ming S. Moy, a Chinese-American engineer. His employment with General Electric took us to Japan for almost four years in the late 1950s. Although I had sworn I would never return, this opportunity to reassess the country from a more mature perspective helped me resolve much of my ambivalence. I made several friends—warm, intimate relationships that helped to erase the pain of my social isolation during the dreary war years. Immersion in the arts and in the everyday hustle of life also gradually softened the old anger and bitterness. In addition to taking classes in various visual arts, I filled in gaps in my earlier Japanese education with tutors and with a Japanese literature class I attended at Waseda University.

Our marriage did not work out, and my husband and I separated in 1963. With the intention of supporting our two children and myself with a career in teaching, I enrolled at Stanford University, where I received an M.A. in Japanese in 1965. The only position available to me after that was at a four-year college in Southern California, for which I chose not to apply. Being aware of the poor air quality there, I felt it would be terrible for my son's asthma.

I worked briefly as a secretary, followed by a short stint as a social worker for the county welfare department. I then entered U.C. Berkeley, graduating with an M.S.W. in Psychiatric Social Work in 1970. I was fortunate to go on to achieve moderate success in my own practice as a clinical social worker here in California, as well as in teaching and training workshops I conducted in Japan.

Like so many other Nisei, I spent years struggling to find a clear cultural identity, feeling neither fish nor fowl. I now believe my youthful experience of living in both countries helped me in the long run to clarify my stance and beliefs. I see that over time I have unconsciously selected from each of my two heritages that which felt right for me. From the Japanese culture I retain a love of grace, elegance, and subtlety in art and literature, as well as devotion to the traditional values of *on* (indebtedness for past favors), *giri* (duty) and *ninjo* (compassion). These elements I somehow integrated with my American regard for candor, assertiveness, and fun and adventure. As a result, I like to think that today I have the best of both worlds.

In the course of writing this memoir I have relived many joys and many sorrows from childhood and adolescence. I am happy to note that most of the wounds of the past have healed. What remains is a deep gratitude for the peace and contentment that are mine today. I also feel blessed for having found those generous, altruistic mentors whose encouragement gave me the hope and confidence to aspire to a college education and a professional career.

Society has changed dramatically from the days of my youth, especially here in multi-cultural and racially diverse Northern California. My children and grandchildren, products of inter-ethnic and inter-racial alliances, are all comfortable in the "melting pot" that is this America. And I? I no longer have to contend with prejudice and discrimination, and thus feel no need to prove myself to anyone but myself. Now I am simply one American citizen who happens to know quite a bit about Japan.

Jean Oda Moy was born in Washington State and spent her early years in Seattle, moving to Japan shortly before the outbreak of World War II. After the war she returned to the United States to attend college. She combined studies in Japanese with a career as a clinical social worker. She practiced in Sunnyvale, California for many years, and also traveled frequently to Japan to teach and train counselors, social workers and psychologists.

She translated three books from Japanese into English, *Tun-huang* (1978), *Chronicle of My Mother* (1982) and *Shirobamba: A Child-hood in Old Japan* (1991), all works by Yasushi Inouye, one of Japan's foremost writers of the 20th century. Her first translation, *Tun-huang*, received the Cultural Award from the Japan Society of Translators, the Japanese branch of UNESCO. All three translations are available in major libraries in the United States.

Made in the USA
Charleston, SC
03 February 2012